BECAUSE
MY DAD DOES

MERV PAYNE

To Ricky
Best Wishes

Merv Payne

This is dedicated to my dad, and to 'dads and lads' everywhere. Anyone can be a father, but being a dad needs work.

ACKNOWLEDGEMENTS

"You should write a book" they said.", "About you, your dad and Millwall", they said. So here it is. Thanks for going on at me, I'm glad I did now. Thanks to my boys Mike and Tom for your efforts in continuing the family Millwall tradition – despite the distraction of Manchester United, and thanks to my wife Anna and daughter Natasha for putting up with it all. I'd also like to thank all the various people who encouraged me not only to do this but to stick at it. You know who you are.

1
MY NAME IS MERV, AND I'M A MILLWALL FAN

I'm a Millwall fan.

Those four words almost sound like a confession, the kind you announce when standing up for the first time at an Alcoholics Anonymous meeting. In all the years I've uttered them, they've been met with various responses, the majority of them coloured by tabloid headlines of stadium riots or grainy news footage of orange seats being hurled through the air. If I was a Manchester United, Chelsea or Arsenal supporter – or even a follower of one of the less fashionable clubs – a Charlton or a Brentford for example – I'm pretty sure I wouldn't have to justify my footballing allegiance immediately after revealing it.

I used to like my stock reply to that question almost as much as its initial response, which never failed to amuse me – most commonly raised eyebrows or the sort of puffing of cheeks that a car mechanic uses to express what a big job your clapped-out banger is going to be to repair. It was one that none of the glory-hunting Liverpool and Nottingham Forest 'supporters' at my south London junior school (who had never clicked through a turnstile in their lives) could match; even the Chelsea and Crystal Palace fans I went to school with couldn't better it for its authenticity:

"I support Millwall, because my dad does."

For me it was as simple as that, I followed football long before it became 'cool', in fact I was often teased at school for going to the football with my dad every other week. One minute I was a 'hooligan' for following Millwall, the next I was 'weird' for going to home games with my dad. Either way it just washed over me because I'd never known any different since my dad first took me when I was seven.

So before we go any further I need to clear up one of the usual assumptions that usually follow my announcement that I'm a Millwall fan. If you think this is going to be one of those football hooligan books with chapter after chapter recalling tales of 'taking ends' back in the good days of the terraces, chasing, and being chased by, rival fans through the streets before and after matches, I'm sorry, it isn't. Don't get me wrong, there's nothing wrong with those books. I've read and enjoyed plenty of them, from Colin Ward's 'Steaming In', to the Brimson brothers' many volumes, but I'm afraid I'm not qualified to add to their legend.

As someone who followed Millwall, a club with one of the most fearsome reputations for football hooliganism in the country, but never became involved in any of the violence, I always found them quite a fascinating insight into the world that I kept very much on the outside of as I hopped on and off the football special trains and coaches and listened to tales of various 'offs' and who ran who, where and when. I've seen discussions on social media about why there aren't any books by or at least about the hooligan element that followed Millwall over the years and the opinion has always been that it is a world that should be left untouched and definitely not documented and I totally agree.

No, this is actually the story of Millwall's 1987-88 season when they won promotion to the First Division (that's the Premier League, kids) for the first time in the club's 103-year history. Well, there's quite a bit besides that to be honest.

If you're now expecting this to be a detailed match-by-match diary with enough statistics, facts and figures to keep John Motson and Martin Tyler in dead-air match-padding for a couple of years, again, I'm sorry. It's an irreverent collection of memories, nostalgia and stories of all the various ways a teenage football fan managed to follow his team to glory in a never-to-be-forgotten season. Well at least that's how it all started. What it turned into was a nine month rollercoaster of emotions, not just on the terraces or in the stands, but between me and my dad, the man responsible for my love of football – and Millwall.

If you're not a Millwall supporter, I reckon you'll still enjoy it. I appreciate I'm not exactly selling this thing right here, and I'm narrowing my target readership down with every passing apologetic paragraph, but it's only fair to warn you. Personally I've always taken an interest in other fans' experiences, so hopefully, whichever team you follow, you'll find plenty to relate to here.

This is, I hope, something that a fan that followed any football club during the late eighties (when football was very different) will relate to and, hopefully be mildly entertained by. It was a time when you could literally rock up at any football ground at a moment's notice, pay three or four quid to get in and stand on a crumbling terrace and watch the fun unfold, both on the pitch and around you in the stands.

But if you're still reading, stick with me, because it's not just a collection of teenage memories following a Third Division football team that suddenly came good one season. It's much more than that. It's a reminder of the days when dads took their sons to the game and got them hooked in the same way they were decades before – something that is sadly all too rare these days. And it's so much more than just an account of one season. In many ways, Millwall getting promoted is almost the sub-plot. Thanks to my dad, I grew up following Millwall and fell in love with football. Without it, I'm not sure my relationship with my dad would have amounted to much and as dramatic as that sounds, I'm probably not alone in saying that. So a final apology for the times when Millwall's battle for the top spots in the 1987-88 season suddenly transports you to a muddy Croydon football field in 1981 or a south west London council estate in the 1970s, trust me, it's all relevant.

2
NOW OR NEVER

On Saturday September 1st 1979 my dad took me to my first football match. It is a rite of passage that has been repeated by millions of fathers and sons before and after, and it was a day that would shape my life forever. Over the course of the nine years that followed that day, football – and in particular Millwall – became the bond between me and my dad. The bond that usually develops from birth between father and son and involves a whole range of stuff had never fully materialised during those first seven years of my life, but as we walked home from The Den after watching Millwall defeat Carlisle United 1-0 in the Third Division, we had both discovered, almost completely by accident, something to share and bring us closer together over the coming years.

I say by accident because my dad had no intention of taking me to the football that day. He'd planned to go alone as he usually did. After a long week at work and a Saturday morning of chores at our south London flat, it was his little treat to himself. He didn't spend the months or weeks leading up to it planning his son's first introduction to his world of the trials and tribulations of following your team, in fact the thought never crossed his mind to take me along. Why would it?

I seemed happy enough sat on the floor of the lounge with the TV on and my toys spread out in front of me, and he didn't really need the aggravation. It's not as if he hadn't made the effort in the past, he'd taken the boy fishing and that was a disaster, so why disturb a contented child and risk ruining his day at the football?

My dad's plans changed the moment he appeared at the kitchen door in his jacket to say goodbye to my mum who was, as she always seemed to be, either up to her elbows in washing up suds, preparing the next meal or wielding a can of Ajax and a cloth.

Dad was hoping for a simple reply to his "See you later then", what he got knocked him back on his heels.

Mum felt it was only fair she had some time to herself – if only to concentrate on more cooking and cleaning, but perhaps in the hope that, without having me constantly pestering her (because all that was on the TV by now was horse racing and my Star Wars and Action Man figures had long since lost their appeal) she just might have a few minutes left at the end of it all to actually sit down.

So I went with Dad, who was convinced I would be even more bored and ruin his afternoon. It had already cost him more money as he'd promised Mum we'd sit down in the grandstand for safety. He hated sitting down, that wasn't the way to watch football he'd always said, but he decided to brazen it out, safe in the knowledge that in two weeks' time he'd be back to going on his own again. Something else he hadn't bargained for that day though was that I'd absolutely love every sight, smell, shout and cheer of it all and be utterly hooked from the moment we turned the corner into Cold Blow Lane.

Over the coming years I would graduate from the sterile seat in the stands to the terraces (in fact the very next game after that first one) and quickly move from my place messing around with the other kids at the front of the terrace blissfully unaware of what was happening on the pitch, up the steps to join my dad among the fans shouting, cheering, singing and jeering their way through the ninety minutes. At first, going to Millwall with Dad was a bit like visiting a sick elderly relative, there was a strong sense of duty about it, and it wasn't much fun. The novelty of that first match had long since worn off and, whilst my understanding of the game was still very basic, I could tell that things weren't going well by the general depressing atmosphere on the terraces. But I had caught the football bug, and I still loved to hear the all-too-occasional roar when a goal was scored, but boos were the more common soundtrack to those bleak afternoons. Gradually however, I paid more attention and started to follow our fortunes more closely with every trip. We'd see early season promotion promise fall, a great escape from relegation, some electrifying cup adventures under the floodlights, great players come and go and finally in 1985 some success: promotion.

It was only a Third Division runner-up place, but it was success, and I had witnessed it, with Dad. We'd stuck by our team through the bad times and good and here was our reward. I quickly recognised, even in my early teenage years, the significance of sharing this with my dad – especially as, outside of watching football there was pretty much nothing else to share.

So I clung to it with all my heart and yearned for more success to enjoy with him. I wanted us to experience something together watching Millwall that he alone had never seen, something that his uncle Harry – who first took him to Millwall back in the early fifties – had been desperate to see in the years he had followed them.

The baton had been passed to me now, I was the third generation of our family to follow Millwall and none so far had been able to enjoy what many football fans could, at some stage of their lives: First Division Football. So getting into the Second Division, six years after my first match, was a start, and it would surely only be a matter of time now? But this was Millwall, where nothing is ever straightforward and if it can go wrong, usually does.

I'll be the first to admit that, to the onlooker, a lot of our problems might seem self-inflicted. According to my dad, it was the crowd trouble at the Ipswich FA Cup match 18 months before he took me for the first time that prevented him from giving me my Millwall baptism sooner, but, knowing Dad as I did, I knew that to be highly unlikely and, in a bizarre way, it was probably my mum who was actually responsible for him taking me to that first match.

We were desperate to see our team in the First Division for the first time, but it felt like such an impossible dream, even being just one division below. Our faces were pressed firmly against the glass on the outside looking in as teams were promoted and enjoyed matches with Liverpool, Manchester United, Arsenal, Everton and Spurs.

Dad was the eternal pessimist, which rubbed off on me a little, but also forced me to at least try and look on the bright side. Every set-back was met with the same words: "They'll never make it to the First Division, not in my lifetime anyway…" usually as we trudged home from the latest defeat.

At the age of fifteen, I felt like time was running out. Yes, I know, crazy thinking for a fifteen-year-old isn't it? But that's the way it is. Dad was approaching 50 which, these days is nothing – the new 40 apparently, but what played on my mind was the fact that both his dad and his uncle Harry had died in their early fifties. I had no reason to think my dad would be the same, but it was stark reminder that life is too short. Surely Dad's life could only be truly fulfilled by seeing his beloved Millwall win promotion to the Promised Land of Division One? That was the kind of single-track my adolescent brain worked on.

It felt like it was now or never, yet at the end of the 1986-87 season, Millwall seemed to be further away from the First Division than they had ever been.

3
OUT OF THE BLUE

Every year, ten teams will celebrate promotion in the English Football League. Those that narrowly miss out may well be promoted next season. It happens every year, and, over time you'd assume that most fans have been able to celebrate seeing their team rise to the next level. So what was so special about 1987-88?

Well, if you, as I did when I started supporting Millwall, believed that promotion was something that every team enjoyed now and then, you will have quickly learned that this isn't the case. You certainly don't form an orderly queue to wait your turn for success in the real football world, yet during the summer of 1987 we had gone from fearing our club may go bankrupt to actually believing this was going to be the year we finally made it to the First Division.

I promised this would be no statistical record, but let me at least put you in the picture: Back in 1987 Millwall Football Club were in a state of turmoil and transformation, having lurched from one crisis to the next in the preceding seven seasons. They could go one of two ways – up, as a result of a financial gamble, or down into a permanent spiral of footballing oblivion. A financial gamble on getting promotion from the Third to Second Division almost ruined the club in 1982. Luckily, George Graham came to the rescue to save them from what looked like almost certain relegation to the bottom division. A miraculous Division Three runners-up spot two seasons later saw the club's fortunes flip almost overnight.

Graham was odds-on to complete the job and get The Lions into the First Division for the first time in the club's 100 year history. But, as is often the story at Millwall, success is punctuated with trouble. The Luton FA Cup riot towards the end of that 1985 promotion run – and further problems when the club were back in the Second Division following the visit of Leeds – saw crippling all-ticket restrictions send home attendances plummeting to around the 3,000 mark.

Also, following the tragic Bradford fire, demands on clubs to bring crumbling ancient stadia up to minimum safety standards meant player budgets were diverted to compulsory ground improvements. The Den had for so long been Millwall's fortress, but by the time the 86-87 season started and Graham had left for Arsenal, it was starting to weigh around their neck as a millstone.

August 1986 saw the club at one of its all-time lowest ebbs. Half of the terracing was closed for repairs, any player worth anything was sold and a new manager brought in that did nothing to raise supporters' hopes.

The appointment of John Docherty after three years of George Graham felt like trading in an expensive sports car for a Robin Reliant. 'The Doc' was appointed and chairman Reg Burr explained how he came with a reputation for building teams on small budgets, which is football chairman speak for: "Strap yourselves in folks, it's going to be a shit season…".

I don't think I've seen such hatred for a manager that I saw as he made his way to the tunnel after a home defeat to Bradford in just his fourth game in charge. Yet, against all odds, he steadied the ship, brought in some cut-price players and by May 1987 Millwall remained a Second Division club.

Behind the scenes things were happening. Burr had appeared on the back page of the local newspaper The South London Press leaning miserably on one of the terrace barriers, cigar in hand wearing a pin stripe suit and a face like smacked arse. The story explained how close the club were to oblivion unless a backer could be found. Just weeks later, those same local sports pages were somewhat more upbeat.

Burr still wore the appearance of Jacob Marley with chronic hemorrhoids, but now he was announcing a sponsorship deal with the local council, and more importantly, fresh investment from new directors.

The thing is we'd heard it all before, and had witnessed a procession of has-beens, overrated also-rans and injury-prone right-offs come and go through The Den doors while the club's bank balance once more plunged into the red. We were promised however that this time was different.

Sure enough, money was quickly put where mouths were. Signings were made. Good signings. Millwall had money to spend – and spend it they bloody-well did.

Kevin O'Callaghan, the winger who scored the only goal on my first ever visit to The Den back in 1979 before leaving for top flight and big screen fame at Ipswich and Escape to Victory with Sylvester Stallone, returned via Portsmouth. Highly rated defender Steve Wood was signed from Reading and Southampton winger George Lawrence joined the party. All we needed now was a striker to partner the raw young talent of Teddy Sheringham up front.

Rumours abound that we'd bid £300,000 (around three times the club's previous transfer record and probably about £5 million today) for Portsmouth striker Micky Quinn. The bid failed, but within two days, that marquee signing arrived and Millwall were announcing that they intended tearing the Second Division a new one – while the rest of the teams were still slapping on after-sun in the Costas.

One of my most vivid memories of the 1987-88 season is of being woken up by my dad to be told we signed Tony Cascarino. It was about 11pm and he'd heard the news on the radio as he got ready for bed. I'd been tucked up for at least an hour. There probably aren't many 15 year olds these days in bed before eleven – in fact most are probably just getting ready to go out at that time, but as a martyr to the early morning paper round which paid for my essential music and football fix, it was one of the few areas in my life where I managed to exercise some discipline.

In his wisdom, Dad decided the best approach for this late night news bulletin was not to switch on my bedroom light, but to slowly enter my room with his torch. Good judgement calls were never Dad's forte – a weakness that I have frustratingly inherited from him and am reminded of when I make similarly bizarre decisions on a regular basis. I call it 'the Charlie Brown effect'. A branch of 'it-seemed-like-a-good-idea-at-the-time-itis'. I remember watching an episode of the brilliant Peanuts cartoon when Charlie was charged with buying the Christmas tree and decided to purchase the most pathetic looking one out of a forest of glorious Swiss Pines for which he was quite rightly lambasted by his squiggly-drawn pals. I remember watching it as a kid thinking: "That's the sort of thing Dad would do…"

So one minute I'm in a peaceful adolescent slumber, the next I'm awoken in terror assuming we're being burgled, only to be told whilst still trying to work out what the bloody hell was happening that "we'd signed Cascarino", after which Dad crept back out of the bedroom leaving me wondering if it had really actually happened at all.

Night terrors aside, the Cascarino signing was proof that Millwall meant business. This was it, our best chance of promotion to the First Division for the first time in our history. As a club, we'd made the largest investment and biggest gamble on finally making the First Division at a time when we looked least likely to do so. Talk about the element of surprise.

The problem was, at least among Millwall fans, we were now *expecting* to go up. Where we'd once been happy with saveloy and pease pudding, we had a taste for caviar. Looking at this team that had been assembled, it was hard to see how anyone could stop us.

Managing expectation in football fans is one thing. Managing it at Millwall is like putting your plonker in the Lion's mouth and giving it an almighty bash on its bonce.

The new signings were unveiled at a club open day where the gates of The Den were flung open for fans to come down and join their new heroes on the pitch as they congregated for the mandatory team photograph. It's quite funny to look back at that day and recall the handful or so that bothered to turn up. Those that did, including me along with a Crystal Palace supporting friend call Tony who tagged along out of curiosity, were treated to very good bit of PR as players mingled with starry-eyed kids, signed bits of paper and posed for photographs.

They then came together in the standard format of tall players at the back, short stuff sat at the front, for the 1987-88 official team group photograph. Every time I've seen that picture over the years I've found it strange to think I was stood there just behind the photographer watching it being taken. Not sure why, it's just that, the whole team photo thing was usually one of the first treats of the new season. The first time you'd usually see it is when it appears in the local newspaper on the eve of the new campaign or the first home match programme of the season. It was a bit like getting an advent calendar being the first real sign that Christmas was on its way. Seeing the team photo announced to me that: "football was back". Witnessing it being constructed and shot a good few weeks before sort of ruined the magic for me in a bizarre way.

A week or so later when I'd managed to get the photos processed at the local Boots I flicked through the batch of slightly blurred snaps of me stood wearing an embarrassed smile next to Tony Cascarino, Teddy Sheringham, Les Briley, Jimmy Carter, Kevin O'Callaghan and George Lawrence and wondered if I was looking at some priceless keepsakes containing future Millwall legends.

Then I looked at the ones of Tony. In a very odd move for a Palace fan, he'd decided to have his picture taken with some of the players too. Before each one he asked me with a whisper who they were as he didn't want to reveal his non-Millwall allegiance. I told him, and then announced as loudly as possible that Tony was a Palace fan just before pressing the button on my 110 camera. It certainly provided some interesting facial expressions and made a nice change from asking them to say "cheese". In a moment of inspiration as I was posing for my picture with Cascarino I said: "say First Division" which got the biggest laugh of the day. The notion that this little football ground could be hosting the likes of Liverpool and Manchester United twelve months later was still the stuff of fun and fantasy. The first real test would come soon, in our first match away to Middlesbrough. I had promised myself I would go to every match, home and away, league and cup, but I knew it was a promise I'd find hard to keep and it would be one that I failed with on day one – thanks to my mum.

Being creatures of habit, my parents insisted on holidaying at the exact same two week period every summer. Whilst he was far from under the thumb, my dad somehow allowed my mum to dictate these dates, and it always seemed to involve missing the first two matches of the football season. For his part, he got to have the final say on the destination. Mercifully in 1987, dad had insisted that the family budget could only stretch to a bed and breakfast in Margate for one week instead of two. Luckily, this would mean the short train ride home would at least see us back to catch the opening match of this season of all seasons with our regular radio/teletext combination that served us so well when we couldn't actually be there.

Obviously, I would much rather have been on the football special to Middlesbrough, but I was grateful that, unlike the previous summer, we didn't miss the first home match altogether. As we sat on one of the first trains out of Margate station that morning with mum quietly grumbling for the fifteenth time about "why we had to leave so bleedin' early" I felt that dad had maybe pulled off a small victory. I also managed to console myself that a tricky trip to Ayresome Park would have seriously depleted my away travel war chest anyway, which was carefully built up with paper round wages, pocket money and managing, yet again, to not spend any of the holiday money which was collected from various relatives before going away.

There really wasn't much to blow your riches on in Margate back in 1987 and the only mildly interesting thing I managed to find to pass the time was to stroll down to the green in front of the train station to watch the Radio One roadshow with Gary Davies. Getting stuck at the top of the Looping Star rollercoaster at the town's infamous Bembom Brothers amusement park was the high point of the break – and was to prove a very fitting metaphor for the football season to come.

Our accommodation was a traditional little bed and breakfast in Dalby Square. I'm reminded of it every time I watch the Only Fools and Horses 'Jolly Boys Outing' episode because they used it as the location for where Del, Rodney and the rest of the gang stayed. It was run by a likeable character called Frank, a middle-aged Londoner and his Pilipino wife, with almost all of the jobs seemingly done by their young son Wendel. He cooked and served the breakfasts, cleaned up and served at the bar in the evening. Frank was a bit of a wheeler dealer and made some extra cash during the week by taking a family of Scots that were staying there on a minibus tour of London. I don't think they were too impressed as I gather they spent most of the day stuck in traffic looking at the back of the tour buses that Frank had decided to follow – and I don't think his knowledge was too great either. I imagined something similar to the roundabout scene in National Lampoon's European Vacation: "Hey look, kids, there's *Big Ben*, and there's *Parliament*." As holidays go, it was pretty much typical of the low-budget fare I'd grown accustomed to as a child. As one of football's eternal pessimists, Dad had already written off our opening day trip to Middlesbrough.

They were freshly promoted from Division Three after almost going out of business a year earlier but had bounced back with a strong team and impressive manager in Bruce Rioch. The reason for my old man's dreary outlook? "We never win there…"

This seemed to be my dad's stock assessment of almost every away game. It was true that Millwall, whilst being quite well known for their resilience at home (having set a record of unbeaten home league games back in the 60s) were almost equally as famous for struggling on their travels. I already had a lengthy list of destinations of doom which I suspected was extended in order to rebuff my requests for Dad to take me, if distance couldn't be used as a reason for non-attendance:

"Dad, we've got Brentford away next week, can we go?"

"Oh I don't know son, we never win there…"

I pointed out to my dad on each occasion we had this similar conversation for various aborted trips that supporting your team wasn't a matter of only going if you thought they would win – otherwise what was the point in us buying season tickets? But he explained that it 'wasn't as simple as that', which is a standard parental response when they can't come up with a reasonable argument for saying "no".

He would elaborate a little by explaining that the financial and emotional investment had to be weighed up with the amount of precious weekend free time lost to the venture. Well, in his words, it was more like:

"They never win there. I ain't spending a fortune going all up there to see us get thrashed and get back home in the middle of the bleedin' night…"

Every away game was 'all up there' to Dad. Admittedly living in south London, most away destinations were, but this didn't stop him delivering this same verdict for my requests for trips to Portsmouth and Brighton, to name but two less northerly destinations. The thing is, he knew exactly where each of the destinations were, and yet took full advantage of my geographical ignorance for as long as he could get away with it. These days I'm proud of my knowledge of where every single league club is in England – not only its county or area, but its relative distance from Millwall, it's a skill born purely out of Dad's insistence on not attending away matches.

Even at 15, travelling away on my own wasn't yet allowed. This season I decided it was going to be different, but for the first day of 1987-88 I had to be content with sitting in my living room with Dad's radio sat in the centre of the room perched on a footstool and the television permanently set to teletext's 'latest scores'.

Let me explain the Saturday ritual of following from afar back in the days before the Internet, social media and up-to-the-minute live updates of all football matches on Sky: With Millwall playing in some far flung outpost and, in my dad's opinion, more important jobs to be done around the house than being on the special train or coach travelling across the country to cheer on The Lions, everything was geared towards being 'in position' in plenty of time for kick-off. While I was on teletext detail (even this not-so-new technological breakthrough was beyond my dad's comprehension) he would plonk one of our old footstools in the centre of the room and perch his radio on it. This wasn't just to obtain optimum reception for the LBC sports show that went around the various grounds featuring London's clubs, it was like a statement.

As a young child before I'd caught the football bug, I'd be playing out or in my room on a Saturday, oblivious to the football drama unfolding across the land and would occasionally enter the living room. There was rarely any point as television ceased to be interesting between the time Swap Shop ended at lunchtime and Jim'll Fix It began around tea time, but I would sometimes aimlessly wander in to see what was going on. I was greeted by my dad who would react with a two-pronged hand reaction: The left hand and index finger would be rushed to his mouth demanding quiet, whilst the right hand would point an explanatory signal to the small transistor radio sat balanced on the footstool in the centre of the room to inform me that absolute silence was required and why. This was of course repeated if my mum entered the room, which she never did.

This was a tradition that continued for as long as my dad remained on this earth. Even the advances of Sky Sports and terrestrial television providing live match update programmes didn't shift him from being sat in front o his radio on a stool. His only acquiesce was to different radio stations who provided better coverage than LBC whose Sportswatch programme went downhill after Jeff Stelling left. Yes, *that* Jeff Stelling. The same man that currently anchors the Sky Sports *Soccer Saturday* programme which brings all the goals as they go in was the voice bringing us news from Orient's match at Doncaster, Brentford's clash with Chesterfield and Millwall's opening day game at Middlesbrough.

It's hard to believe that, with all that has happened in football over the last thirty years, there is still one thing linking the two very different worlds.

So with Dad poised over the radio, and me staring at the ever-changing Division Two latest score screens on the TV, we created a fairly odd composition against the backdrop of our typical suburban south London sitting room.

Teletext was the Internet of the eighties. Laughably now, back then its luminous clunky graphics brought a previously unheard of immediacy to the holy grail of football fans: latest scores. Pages were accessed by a three digit number from your TV remote which you quickly knew off by heart – 140 for the football index, 142 for the latest Division Two scores. These numbers were often infuriatingly changed at the start of each football season after the pages had been taken out of commission for the summer break. Each division's latest score pages could only fit three or four fixtures on – to allow room for the scorers underneath as and when they happened. The three or four pages of latest scores flicked from one to another at a set interval, which could seem excruciatingly slow if you were waiting for your team's score to appear and elicit the shout:

"Is it stuck? It hasn't moved off that page for ages, type the number in again…"

This would prompt you to key the three digits in again to 'reload' the page, which would appear, refreshed, on exactly the same set of latest scores.

ılarly old TV on rental from DER and the teletext system
ly loud and shrill 'BEEP' each time you pressed a button. It
:hed you could clearly hear it above everything else all over
the ... relationship with this particular medium would become a
love-hate one and lead me to make late evening phone calls of complaint to
their HQ and break light fittings, but more about that later.

I did mention to my dad on various occasions that the radio was now surely
redundant and it would make far more sense for us to be both sat staring at
the flickering television screen, but he remained steadfastly loyal to his
transistor pocket-sized pal. My point seemed valid though when, while he
was still hearing how close Gillingham or someone equally irrelevant had
come to taking the lead against whoever they were playing, I watched the
page change to reveal a 28th minute Teddy Sheringham goal had given us
the lead. Muted celebrations ensued, knowing that with only a third of the
match gone, there was plenty of time for this to turn sour. It was a lead that
would last until fifteen minutes from time and the usual fears that an
equaliser would inevitably lead to ultimate defeat didn't materialise leaving
us with a respectable draw.

There are varying degrees of despair when it comes to seeing your team
concede. The ultimate, at the suicidal end of the spectrum, is obviously late
in a crucial match, say a last minute goal in a cup final, vital promotion or
relegation six-pointer or to take a giant-killing away from you at the last
gasp. Conceding any significant goal at home comes next. There's no worse
sound than that distant echo of the away fans' goal celebrations. It's
particularly hard to take if the visitors have brought a large following but
feels bizarrely worse when it's eight blokes and an umbrella leaping about
the away end in muted delirium. After that, watching your team concede –
even if you're 5-0 up – leaves a very slight but inescapable sick feeling the
pit of your stomach.

Television provides a very faint filter against all this, but as Millwall were
never on TV back in the 80s, it wasn't something I'd had experience of.

Hearing your defence breached over the airwaves during latest score round-up programmes is on the next notch of the scale.

I think it's the matter-of-fact way it is broadcast:

"Goal at Deepdale where Preston have equalised against Millwall and at Ashton Gate it's now Bristol City two, Grimsby nil…"

It's like being handed a parking ticket when you return to your car by a traffic warden who simply moves on to the next vehicle and processes another fine, ignoring your genuine argument for being illegally parked.

Nowadays, on the television score update shows, it's done with a well-planned essence of theatre, where the anchor will announce with Shakespearian gravitas:

"Millwall fans have had to endure four home matches without witnessing their team score a goal, that's over six barren, goalless hours down there in south east London. Well, I can tell you, there's been a goal at The Den , but the big question is, has that home drought for The Lions ended? (BIG DARAMATIC PAUSE) …I'm afraid it hasn't, Gary Cotterill is here to tell us about more misery for Millwall…"

Stelling is the master of this, although sometimes he overdoes it and has his thunder stolen by the vidiprinter popping the score up beneath him before he is able to complete his monologue and handover. Farce is never far away in the Sky Sports Saturday studio either when Stelling is attempting to impart another mind-blowing list of statistics about Morecambe's remarkable feat of having a goal scored by a player whose surname begins with the letter 'T' in each of their last eight away league games only to be interrupted by a shout of "GOAL" or "PENALTY" by one of his co-presenters.

Teletext offered no such theatre, not even the briefest of descriptions. Just the goal scorer and goal time in light blue type beneath the team you're playing against and then on to the next page.

The final act is for the letters 'FT' to appear next to your match signaling it's all over. Then, within a matter minutes you've seen all the final scores – few of which are a surprise as you've seen most of the goals go in anyway, the radio and footstool are stashed away and it's almost as if nothing happened. None of the ritual of walking from the stadium to dissect the afternoon's events with fellow fans, wondering how other teams have fared, catching the odd result on a passing car radio as you make your way home and then pouring over the results.

Obviously nothing beats being there.

4
THE GREAT ESCAPE

Victor Frederick Payne – my dad – was born in Camberwell, south London in October 1938 to parents Fred and Ivy. Brother Terry came along five years later and they were brought up in Peckham where their first family home was at Acorn Place before moving to Blenheim Grove. Dad left school at 15 and took a course in building and bricklaying which enabled him to join the family painting and decorating business run by his dad and uncle Harry. For a few years life was good and Dad was blissfully happy living at home, working through the week, enjoying a few pints in the Prince Albert pub on Friday night and walking to The Den to watch Millwall on Saturday. He would have been perfectly happy to repeat that simple little routine for the rest of his life.

Terry meanwhile left home to start a family of his own. Life changed suddenly however when Fred suffered a massive stroke and was confined to a wheelchair. The business, which was already starting to suffer, collapsed completely. Dad looked after him until he died two years later in 1969 and then took various temporary jobs as a labourer. He decided it was time to strike out on his own – on a personal level at least – and signed up to a dating agency. He was matched with Gwen, a woman three years his junior from nearby Balham, who had also just lost her father. They met for the first time in The Bank of Swans pub in Clapham and, after a second date, my dad proposed and they were married 12 months later in 1971.

It was, even by their own admission, something of a marriage of convenience. Both had been left to care for their mothers after their fathers had died, with their siblings all starting families of their own. Both had decided to find companionship for later life rather than face it alone. Hobson's Choice 1970s style. Dad was still in between jobs, doing the odd shift on various building sites here and there so money was in short supply. Dad moved in to the Balham flat with Gwen and her mum. Living with your in-laws was nothing new in those days. Dad's mum wasn't exactly overjoyed with the arrangement but had since re-married. Life quickly settled down, until I came along.

For me, like most children, growing up was all about escape. From the age of five I was free to roam the large sprawling concrete and grass paradise that was my home: The Weir Road Estate in Balham. I loved to wander between the large beige-coloured blocks of flats with their bright blue-painted doors and listen to the echo of my voice shouted in the stone stairwells.

My adventures around the estate often had a soundtrack, provided by one of the many radios that residents had perched on kitchen or bathroom window-ledges alongside the washing up liquid, bleach and Ajax bottles. On warm weekend afternoons I could take in any number of different tunes wafting from open windows or doors as I made my way around the estate's seven blocks.

Back home, the radio enabled me to completely lose myself in music and by the age of six I was regularly scribbling down a song title and artist on a scrap of paper and handing it to my mum along with my crumpled one pound note pocket money before we left for the Monday morning school run. She would then visit the record counter of Woolworths on Balham High Road as part of her regular weekly shop and purchase my single request.

The first one was "Take Me I'm Yours" by Squeeze. She braved the embarrassment she said she felt asking for such titles as this, along with

"Hit Me With Your Rhythm Stick" by Ian Dury and The Blockheads and "Making Plans For Nigel" by XTC and I always arrived home from school to find the single in its little white paper Woolworths bag ready to play, and play it I did, reveling in this wonderful new world.

I seemed to find trouble almost constantly in my first year of school. I wasn't a bad child. I never fought – to this day I have never actually hit someone in my 46 years of being on this earth – but as I was quick to become bored, my natural instinct to fight routine or the norm engendered a dangerous creativity, more commonly known as 'getting up to mischief'. It ranged from filling up one of Gordon McCrudden's slip-on school shoes at the playground water fountain to constantly being caught running on the grass – which was strictly forbidden at my infants school.

As a result, I found myself receiving the regulation punishment for five-year-old school miscreants: a lunchtime in the headmistress's office.

Back in the seventies, most schools took the same name but their infants and junior sections were completely separate and had their own head teachers. The head of my school – Glenbrook Infants in Clapham – was Miss Austin. She was a formidable figure. She looked, dressed and acted like one of those classic actresses from the old black and white films my mum used to watch on Sunday afternoons.

Anyone misbehaving was sent to her office at lunchtime after finishing their dinner. They were not accompanied, you had to go on your own, knock on the door and explain why you were there. She would then admonish you and lead you to the wall opposite her desk. On this wall was a large calendar – the sort of wall planner you get in big offices. A red plastic ball-shaped pin was fixed in the current day. Miss Austin ordered you to stand up facing the calendar with your nose touching the wall. She took the pin from its spot, and replaced it at the spot your nose touched the wall. You then had to remain perfectly still with your nose touching the red plastic back of the pin until such time she deemed your punishment was complete. While you did this, she would be busying herself at her desk, which was always shrouded in smoke which wafted up from her cigarette which she dragged on from a long fancy black and gold holder. This was then placed into an equally fancy stand – which looked like the ones you see holding pens on chains in banks.

I can remember the feeling of panic and desperation the first time I was eased against that wall. A flurry of anxiety was coursing through my brain, making my legs weak and my stomach sick. I wanted it to stop and the longer it went on the more I panicked. When it was finally over she asked me to step back and it was then that it dawned on me. I looked again at the large calendar laid out in front of me with its 365 days. They were all empty white boxes, with just one exception: the one where I had been pressing my nose against the pin. The insignificance of it all quickly occurred to me. This was just one little pin in a whole expanse of blank spaces. There was no need for me to panic about it. A voice in my head was gently but efficiently coaxing me back to confidence again. I can still hear it to this day telling me: "It's not the end of the world" and it worked a treat. Without realising it, I had come up with my own way of dealing with my hang ups and putting them into perspective.

I suppose things could have gone one of two ways from there. This might have galvanised me to become immune from punishment or retribution and led to a life of trouble and crime. Fortunately, I decided on the reverse course of action, thanks mainly to my new teacher. Mrs Rejko was of Panamanian descent, spoke with an exotic accent and was very abrupt in her manner, never one to sugar coat anything – even to her six-year-old class pupils. She specialised in Art and one day we were drawing away happily when I was aware of her presence at my shoulder.

"No, no, no, that's WRONG!" she exclaimed, picking up my picture of a boat bobbing along on top of the ocean.

"The boat is IN the water, not on TOP OF IT!" and she quickly scribbled a new craft with the sea meeting the horizon behind it. I instantly saw it and was amazed.

"Quick, draw me a house" she hustled.

"Er, what sort of house?" I offered

"A house, a house, ANY house, a door, four windows and roof A HOUUUUSSSE" her eyes bulged as she stretched the word out.

I quickly drew the mandatory 'Play School' house, the flat square with oblong door, four square windows and a triangle roof.

"OK" she said, her voice calming. "Now try it like this"

She took my pencil from me and then added the sides to my house and roof to make it 3D, then redrew the exact same house in perspective. I was gobsmacked.

"That's amazing" I chirped. She smiled at me and handed the pencil back.

"Perhaps you would like to spend your lunchtimes in my art class rather than Miss Austin's office, then you might learn something?"

So that was that. I became obsessed with drawing and when I wasn't drawing I was listening to music and when I wasn't listening to music I was making sure I had something to fill in all the gaps that life presented me with. It's what most children learned to do before they were able to spend their days staring at an iPad or laptop. What we sometimes don't realise is that, even in adult life there are gaps in life. These are gaps that are much harder to fill with such positive energy, and this is what my dad struggled with, although I couldn't possibly see this as a child.

Everyone from time to time wants to escape. For as long as I can remember I wanted to get away from something. As a bored five-year-old I wanted to escape the monotony of quiet Sunday afternoons with nothing on three television channels worth watching. I wanted to escape the four walls of the classroom which prevented me from enjoying myself. Later in life I wanted to escape the morning commute, the nine-to-five drudgery and monthly slavery to pay my way. Like most young men I found it in the usual places: music, friends, girlfriends and of course football. Dad had introduced me to a whole new world of escape, one you could share with thousands of like-minded people young and old. The focal point of this escape was The Den.

There is no more idyllic scene for me than a football stadium at the start of the football season. Clicking through the turnstiles on an August afternoon, your senses bombarded with those familiar sights, sounds and smells that have been missing since May would actually send a shiver down my spine. I'd completely forgotten how much I'd taken it for granted, and how much I'd missed it.

Pushing through those turnstiles was the ultimate form of escapism for me. I could leave all my problems outside those big blue gates. It was my Narnia. Upsets at home or at school were abandoned and forgotten, like coats left to be looked after at a theatre and collected afterwards when the show had ended. I stood on the Millwall terraces and watched my team and that's all that mattered.

The first home game was always bathed in warm sunshine. Of course it was. Just like every summer holiday as a child. The reality was almost certainly very different, but the memory is far kinder. Even a stadium like The Den, which had seen far better days, appeared gleaming and clean. Its terraces packed with shirt-sleeved tanned arms using match programmes as sun visors, leaning on what appeared to be freshly painted bright yellow crush barriers shining in the late summer afternoon glare.

I quickly realised that, just like the team we watched in it, Millwall's ground was inferior in many ways to the others elsewhere in the country. Watching Match of the Day or The Big Match, I marveled at the huge packed cantilever stands of Old Trafford and the vast swaying terraces at Highbury. We had nothing like that at Millwall. A small crumbling concrete bowl on three sides, with only half covered by an aging roof whose supports would obscure the view of the unlucky ones on rainy days. Its decrepit state had seen its capacity reduce from almost 50,000 to around 15,000. But from day one I realised three things: This team wasn't very good, its stadium wasn't very good, but they were *mine* – and that was all that mattered.

The first home game always had a buzz about it, but on this first league visit to The Den in August 1987, the place was humming like a nuclear reactor ready to blow. The expectancy was as pungent in the air as the whiff of roll-up cigarette smoke and burger-stand onions. The previous Saturday's actual season opener was seen as nothing more than a dress rehearsal. That was merely Wilbur and Orville kicking the tyres, giving the prop a quick spin and oiling the engine. Right here, right now, at The Den, we'd see if this thing could actually fly.

The carnival atmosphere, which often disappeared by half time at most of Millwall's opening home games of the season, thankfully lasted long into the early evening. Even the hardened Den cynics who observed that every expensive high-profile signing the club had ever made was doomed to failure, would have been encouraged by Cascarino's opener in the comfortable 3-1 win. It was an expected win though and those first two matches of the season, frustration away and dominance at home would pretty much set the scene for the first part of the season. If Millwall were finally going to make it to the First Division, they'd have to start winning away from The Den, and that would have to start the following week at Leicester, mainly because that was going to be my first 'proper' away trip.

I'd gone through the usual charade with Dad when planning this trip:

"Dad, do you fancy going Leicester? It's only six quid for the coach."

I'd taken the expense element out of the argument from the start, and in truth it was £6 for me but £8.50 for him as he wasn't a member of the away travel club. It that was a subsidy I felt I could afford, but he still had history on his side:

"Leicester? Cor, can't remember the last time we won there, all that way on a poxey coach to see 'em get turned over? I don't think so."

At least I hadn't simply got the "They never win there…", usually delivered without so much as glance up from his paper or over the rim of him black national health spectacles which made him look a bit like Reggie Kray – well the top bit of his head visible over his Daily Mirror anyway.

No, this time, I'd got some attention, he'd put the paper down and elaborated. It was the Shep Pettibone 12 inch remix of "We never win there", but it was progress.

Travelling on my own was still not allowed, but this season I had several plan Bs in place. One of them was Steve. Away trips with older friends was considered safe and Steve was as keen as me to take in as many matches as possible this season – even though learning to drive was his number one priority and meant that funds were tight.

I'd already bought the tickets before the conversation with my dad had taken place. Buying tickets or away travel for matches back in 1987 wasn't the same painless, virtually instantaneous ecommerce experience it is today. At Millwall, it had to be done before, at half time or after a previous home match, or, as I preferred, during the week.

Even in the eighties, most football stadiums had club shops and ticket offices. The club shops resembled shops and the ticket offices were – well offices where you walked in to a customer-friendly environment and you were served what you wanted. At Millwall it was very different. The club shop was almost a hole in the wall. It was nothing more than an opening on the outside of the Cold Blow Lane end of the ground, next to the main gates and turnstiles where fans and players alike entered the stadium. You walked into the small entrance and edged your way along the windowless tunnel, choosing what you wanted from the wares pinned to the wall behind the makeshift counter.

Once paid for, you continued along to the end where Jimmy Flannagan had his little programme section next to the exit door and made your way out into the street again. This was only open on match days. Tickets for away games were purchased by walking up to the small office window situated behind the Cold Blow Lane terrace which faced you as you entered the turnstiles. This office was usually manned by Billy Neil, who had played for the club in the sixties and was a fan favourite before injury cut short his career.

Billy would take care of most of the commercial activities and my dad still found it fascinating that such a prestigious ex-player would be stood at that little window handing out tickets. I suppose it's a bit like turning up at Old Trafford to buy something from the club shop and being served by Ryan Giggs.

Usually, if I needed to get something from the ticket office I'd pop in as soon as we arrived at the ground. As we pushed our way through the turnstile and emerged on the little crowded forecourt of the Cold Blow Lane end, I'd announce to Dad that I needed to pop to the office and would meet him on the terrace if there was a queue. More often than not he would insist on coming with me and while Billy was serving me, just stand there staring with a strange smile on his face like a teenager with a silly crush on next door's grown up daughter. He just couldn't get his head around the idea that this terrace idol from his youth was now merely flogging tickets out of a little window.

On non-match days, pretty much all football stadiums were closed to the public. Like Willy Wonka's factory, they'd be a hive of mysterious midweek activity inside, safely protected from the public by large club-coloured, crest-emblazoned metal gates. Not Millwall. Because of their lack of external facilities, the large blue barriers on Cold Blow Lane were open all week. You could just stroll up and wander around the ground and, as odd as that might sound, many did. The sight of an empty football stadium is really quite enduring.

I liked nothing better in the school holidays than taking the train to New Cross Gate and walking that same route to The Den, enjoying the almost spooky solitude without the usual match day crowd striding purposely in the same direction. Then I'd walk into the ground, approach the little office and, reaching through the bars on the window, tap on the glass. Various voices could be heard coming from the other side – the loudest being the unmistakable Scottish tones of Billy, which would increase in volume as he approached the window and flung it open with a smile and a cheery greeting. This was how away tickets were bought. They were usually fished out of a tatty cardboard box or old green file and exchanged for your cash after showing the necessary documentation – season ticket or away travel club membership. It was a bit like having your credentials scrutinised at check point Charlie, only by a far friendlier Scottish bloke rather than a stern German soldier.

Once I had safely stashed my tickets, the pilgrimage was completed by mounting the steps to the Cold Blow Lane terrace entrance. Appearing at the top and getting that first glimpse of the lush green Den turf without the noise of the crowd was a strangely calming experience. There always seemed to be something going on, whether it was the distant noise of some repair work being done somewhere in the bowels of the main stand, or the hypnotic hiss of a hosepipe watering the pitch. Occasionally there would be players doing training or recuperation exercises in the days before clubs owned out-of-town training facilities and gyms. On one occasion I watched John Docherty and his assistant Frank McLintock go through some set piece routines with a few players before a suited man holding a microphone accompanied by a cameraman emerged from the players' tunnel next to the goal and interviewed Docherty for the local news. After a short question and answer session, Docherty led his players back down the tunnel, leaving the interviewer who thanked him for his time and then, turning to his cameraman said:

"Right, shall we do some nods now?"

The cameraman then filmed the interviewer nodding attentively and pulling various expressions of interest while holding his mic poised for the next answer. These were obviously cut into the interview at the editing stage later, meaning the cameraman didn't have to swing from one talking head to another. It was my first lesson in the strange and deceptive world of TV. I felt strangely cheated.

This ritual of visiting an empty football terrace wasn't exclusive to me. I would quite often be joined by three or four other fans that would stroll onto the terrace and sometimes sit down on the steps – possibly in their usual match day place – and just stare at the pitch. It was almost like finding a handful of parishioners sat in their church in quiet personal contemplation and was just one of the pleasures lost when Millwall moved to their new stadium in 1993.

I spent an entire afternoon and money on a train ticket to get my hands on two coach tickets to Leicester. These days I go to the club website, log in to my account, choose my tickets and pay with my card. It's a sterile, joyless process that takes approximately three minutes. I know which method I prefer, and I miss it every time I buy a ticket for a match.

I'd known Steve since I was nine. We'd met playing for the worst football team in the world. That's not an exaggeration. Norwood United really were the worst team in the world, having gone almost an entire season without scoring a single goal and racking up some truly horrendous defeats, starting with a 33-0 reverse on my first ever properly organized football match. The club was run by Mick and Ray, two well-meaning chaps who lived on a local estate and were keen to organise sporting events to keep the kids out of trouble.

Mick's wife Marion was the local childminder and had a heart of gold. Transport was provided by Mick's transit van which he drove all over the Croydon area with thirteen junior footballers of ridiculously varying ages squashed into the back on the wooden bench seats that flanked the vehicle's dusty interior. We would all spill out of the back of the van outside Mick's house after another heavy loss, greeted by Marion at the door with a cheery "How did you get on lads? 15-0? Oh well never mind, it's better than last week, you'll get there". Bless her.

I'm not sure exactly what I grew tired of first, the double-figure humiliations or the constant re-enactment of the McCain Oven Chips TV ad on both the outward and return journey in that bloody van. Every time I see a transit now I hear "Hope it's chips, it's chips, we hope it's chips, it's chips…" and Mark Smith's awful West Indian accent which sounded more like Welsh as he insisted doing the "fried onion rings" bit.

It was while we were once again being disconsolately decanted from the team bus that a tall skinny ginger boy who I'd chatted to briefly at some of the matches shoved past me and immediately turned to apologise.

"Sorry mate, I'm in a hurry, I'm going to watch the football with my dad and I'm late." And with that he disappeared down the road.

"Don't bother Steve, Millwall are shit!" came the call from inside the van.

I was in the same situation. Millwall had started playing home games on Sundays in an effort to boost flagging attendances and I had to get a move on if I was to make it home in time to make the match with my dad.

We'd moved from my Balham home in south west London when I was seven. Balham was about the same distance in either direction from Chelsea, who all my family on my mum's side supported, and Millwall – which was my Peckham-born dad's family's team of choice. Mercifully I chose Millwall, but we now lived in South Norwood – just a few streets away from Crystal Palace's Selhurst Park stadium and the area was almost entirely Palace fans. I kept my Millwall allegiance to myself, assuming no one in the area would be a fan but once I learned that Steve and his dad were Lions fans too, we quickly became friends, our chats about what was going on down at The Den kept us warm as we stood on the side-lines taking our turns as Norwood United subs.

The team understandably disbanded after just one season in 1983, the same year that I started high school, and the same one that Steve attended – but two years above me. He and his dad stood on the halfway line at Millwall, whereas my dad always preferred to stand behind the goal in the Cold Blow Lane end. Each home game, we would meet up before kick-off at the bottom of the terrace next to the large yellow metal railings that divided the two banks of crumbling concrete to discuss all things Millwall. We also worked at the same newsagents, on the early morning paper rounds, where there was a troop of about six of us doing various routes. My friendship with Steve gave me access to a priceless commodity at high school: acceptance by the older kids. I'd often see Steve at school or on the way there in the morning and he was happy to chat to me about Millwall rather than being embarrassed to be seen talking to a kid two years below him and this in turn saw me strike up some rather tentative friendships with his mates too. This sort of thing can prove very handy in the bearpit-like atmosphere of an inner city 1980s secondary school. It's a bit like having Crocodile Dundee along with you on a tour of the Outback.

With my dad's expected refusal to go to Leicester, Steve was a grateful recipient of his ticket. And so we found ourselves stood outside a school close to The Den at 8am on a Saturday morning waiting for the coach. We were soon joined by a small crowd of quiet, mostly hungover fellow fans, older ladies dressed in far too many clothes for the time of year, and Lottery Larry.

Lottery Larry was a tall, thin, middle-aged man with a toothy smile who travelled to every single away game, selling the club's lottery tickets. Hence the nickname. Larry wasn't his real name of course, this was used purely for alliterative purposes and, in the true sense of nicknames, no-one really knew what his real name was – apart from his closest friends and family. His other instantly recognisable feature was his Parka coat which he wore whether it was 80 degrees in August or freezing in December. I don't mean to be disrespectful here, it's just the only way I can describe him. I love people like Lottery Larry. Every club has them. Fans who dedicate all their lives to following their team but also helping out and being as much a part of it as they can. People who don't know what Millwall is really like would probably be amazed to meet people like Lottery Larry, a loyal, conscientious and knowledgeable fan who loves his club, following Millwall. There are still people to this day that assume following Millwall away is like a scene from A Clockwork Orange.

As the coach arrived, the silence was broken.

"What the FUCK is THAT?!" a voice barked, followed by hollow laughter.

A battered old blue coach which looked as though it was on its first excursion since ferrying evacuees during the war trundled to a halt at the roadside and its doors clattered open with an unconvincing hiss.

"This thing is falling apart" Steve giggled as we took our seats. He wasn't that far off.

About half way into the journey the coach hit a bump on the M1 which wouldn't have even been noticed by a vehicle with something resembling suspension. For this shaky charabanc however, it was as if it had been driven into a fallen tree and shook everyone out of their seats. Just as we thought the turbulence had ended a loud crash came from the front of the coach as the large round clock that was fixed into the front of the cab fell out and smashed on the floor next to the driver.

Somehow we arrived at Leicester in one piece and after being escorted by Police through the rugby ground we were left at what looked like a far inferior stadium in Filbert Street. Pumped up, not just for the match but at the sheer thrill of surviving the coach journey from Hell, kick off approached and the teams emerged one at a time from the tunnel.

"Yes come on boys!" Steve let out a bellow and clapped his hands loudly. Instantly I was aware of every pair of eyes in the away end glaring at us. Unaware, Steve turned to me.

"Come on, why aren't you cheering?" he asked.

Dumfounded, I replied, ashen faced:

"Because that's Leicester coming out of the tunnel Steve…"

Steve instantly clapped his hand over his mouth then his face and thankfully the glares turned to giggles as he realised his mistake.

"Shit, I saw the blue shirts and thought it was Millwall!" he exclaimed horrified.

The trauma of that coach journey was clearly still taking its toll.

To make matters worse, Steve spent the time that Millwall emerged from the tunnel in their change kit of all red explaining to me, and anyone else who would listen, the reasons why he'd mistakenly cheered the opposition, while we all greeted the team.

The match didn't improve matters. A very poor Leicester side won the game with the only goal. It was one of those matches where, as soon as the first goal goes in, you know that's going to be it. Millwall were poor, and the few touches that Cascarino had were greeted with chants of "what a waste of money" from the fans of the club that had been one of those rivalling Millwall for his signature.

The verdict as we walked back to the coach was typically damning.

"Cascarino's crap", "he's not up to this division, he can't play with Sheringham", "Sheringham's too lazy, can't be bothered…"

As we took our seats on the coach, talk shifted from whether or not this team was up to the task of getting us promoted to whether the beleaguered bus we'd boarded was up to the job of getting us home. As it chugged through the busy town centre traffic, a fan listening to the results coming through on his radio piped up:

"Gillingham won 8-1"

It was true. Gillingham, the team who were supposed to be wondering where the next goal was coming from after selling their top scorer Tony

Cascarino to us in the summer had scored eight. Meanwhile, Cascarino had mustered barely a shot in anger all day. Gallows humour followed about how we'd 'been done over' by the Kent club and then moved on again as the coach hit the open road to which part of it would fall off next. We didn't have long to wait.

There was a strange sense of irony as we watched the large pane of glass bounce down the hard shoulder of the M1. It had popped out without warning from the window two rows down from us and, clearly made of stronger stuff than the rest of the coach, boinged a few times on its rubber seal edge before coming to rest in the grass verge. Without any reaction, the driver continued, leaving us to have extra ventilation for the rest of the journey.

"Well the wheels have come off Millwall, and the window's come off the coach" someone announced drily from the back. It was still only August, but what little patience Millwall fans possess quickly dissipates.

As I arrived home late that Saturday evening, Dad's head poked out of the living room before I had chance to shut the front door behind me.

"I told you we never win there" he chirped, almost sounding happier to have been proved right than if we'd have managed a win. This was partly true of course; he'd have been overjoyed to have heard that we had snatched an unlikely three points while he listened along on the radio that day, but secretly gutted to have knocked back the chance to see it in the flesh. I could sense a tinge of admiration from him though. This was the first time I'd travelled some distance to follow our team and whilst I was downbeat I was unbowed, I would do it again, of course I would, and sooner or later, one way or another, I'd make sure I took Dad with me.

5
SPLODGEGUN

Dad was a completely different person from the moment we left our house on our way to a match. The walk to the station was filled with excited chatter about what the game might bring; the opposition, who played for them, where they were from, what sort of team they were. Dad amazed me with his knowledge of other teams and their players and I couldn't get enough of his little potted histories about the Carlisles, Chesters and Gillinghams.

He seemed to have an anecdote from his Millwall-supporting youth about them all. Every moment of the journey to the game was filled with question and answer sessions which Dad was happy to indulge. There was a sparkle in his eye as he recalled games from years before, players who had left Millwall for that day's opponents and would be bound to shine, or the star performers that we had to keep an eye on. It was as if a switch had been flicked somewhere.

The most noticeable energy of Dad's enthusiasm was in nostalgia. Taking me to Millwall was clearly a form of regressive therapy for him, although I obviously didn't see that at the time. At the match he was even more animated, shouting, singing and swearing. Dad was old school. He never swore at home. The closest he came was a prolonged "FFFFFFFFFFF..." when an old-fashioned look from my mum was enough to curtail the remaining three letters from escaping his mouth.

At the football however it was open season. There's something very funny about hearing someone swear when you're not used to it. Some might frown upon this and say that he was exposing me to bad language at too tender an age, but I knew the rules, this was his world, it was allowed.

I was surrounded by thousands of mostly male voices aggressively cursing, shouting and singing their way through ninety minutes of football. This foul-mouthed gravel-voiced choir would be conducted by events on the pitch: a near miss, a bad tackle, a poor refereeing decision, all drawing varying crescendos of "oooh", "aaaah", "fuck off number nine" and "you blind wanker ref…" Me and Dad – just like most of the other kids and their dads – had an unwritten agreement.

This is where men are allowed to swear, you don't copy it, and you certainly don't breathe a word of it back home. What goes on at the football stays at the football. Which is fine as far as the swearing is concerned, but it's a rule that opens up a whole new sinister world, which I'll come to shortly.

One of the funniest things I saw my dad do at football was to join in with a chant of "Where were you in fucking Spain" aimed at the Cardiff fans during the build up to our first home match of the 1982-83 season. The chant was clearly mocking Wales' lack of involvement in that summer's World Cup. I'd never seen my dad join in any terrace chants and I was both shocked and impressed in equal measure. Equally so when, later in the game which Cardiff were running riot in and would go on to win 4-0, a small group of young men behind us tried in vain to start up a chant of "Aberfan, Aberfan" mocking the 1966 disaster when almost an entire village was wiped out after a coal tip landslide claimed the lives of 28 adults and 116 children in the little Welsh mining community.

Dad was very much the "don't get involved" type who always chose to avoid confrontation – especially in public – the sort of bloke who would go out of his way to avoid eye contact with someone smoking in the non-smoking carriage of a train and never dare tell them to put their cigarette out, but instead flick knowing glances at his fellow passengers in the hope they were brave enough to say something. But this was different, we were at the football. Dad spun around, glared in the direction of the chanters and let rip:

"That's fucking disgusting, kids died, hundreds of people died, you're a fucking disgrace, shut it NOW!"

Time stood still for what felt like an age. The action on the pitch suddenly dissipated into the background. This could turn nasty and as brave as Dad was with his words, I knew he wasn't a fighter – especially up against half a dozen young men. To my amazement they backed down. With support for my dad's outburst coming from behind and either side of their group they skulked off to the bar at the back of the stand. I was in awe, but made to promise that no word of it would reach my mother's ears. Of course it wouldn't, it would stay safely behind the big blue gates after the final whistle.

The last remnants of those magical few hours with Dad would flicker away over our evening meal which was always on the table when we arrived home from the match. We would dissect the afternoon's events, carefully edited to avoid any bad behaviour and gradually, over the pork chops, carrots and gravy, Dad would slowly return to his previous self. The conversation would gradually turn to every day matters between him and Mum. The lustre faded from his face and my questions were once more met with an irritated response like a troublesome fly.

We returned to our separate corners for the rest of the week, until the next match, Dad would revert to the distant character that I was more accustomed to. I was so desperate to have that Dad from the Millwall terraces at home with us. Surely Mum would excuse the odd swear word here or there if it meant having a more animated Dad around the house? But of course Mum didn't see the transformation that I saw and didn't crave the attention that I did.

There had to be another way.

By the age of eight I was keen to extend my love of watching football to playing. I had quickly grown tired of blasting my ball against the fence on the large patio in our shared garden, although I doubt I was anywhere near as weary of this as our neighbours were. The ball made a satisfying 'THWACK' on the freshly-creosoted panels and I spent hours trying to master the age-old technique of belting the ball at various speeds and trajectories and trapping it perfectly, ready to swivel Kenny Dalglish-style at a ninety degree angle to face down the long garden before aiming my match-winning shot at goal. Whilst the hapless on-coming defenders were part of my imagination, surging toward me from the rose bush borders to try and block my shot, I was lucky enough to have an actual goal to aim for.

Well OK it wasn't a goal as such. The single mum who lived in the top floor flat had two daughters. Their dad would make occasional visits to see them and go through all the usual rituals: trips to McDonalds, the zoo, London Dungeons etc, and of course the 'guilt present'. This would be an extravagant gift for both of them at birthdays or Christmas. I think these included an Atari games console, a full size keyboard – and gloriously for me – a large set of swings. I sat watching him assemble the large green metal structure at the end of the garden one afternoon and as he tried to impress me with the two swings and a strange sort of see-saw pergola ride thing which had two seats, all I could think of was: "That's going to make a cracking set of goal posts".

My afternoons were therefore complete. I would carefully hang both swings up out of the way and the see-saw pergola thing (which was rigid metal bolted to the frame and couldn't be moved) made for a perfect goalkeeper. OK so his positioning left a lot to be desired as he was always way over to the right of his goal, but on the occasions when my shot accuracy wasn't on point and I couldn't find the vacant left side of the 'net', watching the ball 'saved' as it pinged back off one of the yellow plastic seats added some realism which I responded to with either clapping both hands to my face in disbelief that my shot had been saved and pushed over for a corner, or a desperate dash to make the rebound and nod it home. There was one other problem with these 'goals' and that was the uprights obviously leant at 45 degree angles, but on the plus side this provided a 'stanchion' which would serve as a fantastic prop for attempts to recreate Clive Allen's infamous 'goal that never was' for Crystal Palace at Coventry.

Like most boys, I was glued to the football on television. Match of the Day and The Big Match were stared at with the same intensity as Top of the Pops. I loved football commentary and this extended to catching games on the radio too which I enjoyed even more. When you watch a game on television there's a tendency to ignore the commentary a little but I was mesmerised at how people like Peter Jones in particular could paint pictures of the matches as you listened, and transfer every detail of the tension and excitement of the match perfectly from the commentary box into your living room. Even at the age of seven and eight I didn't assume this was easy – even though they made it sound so. I could tell straight away that this was an immense talent – and a fascinating extension to the world of story-telling that I loved so much.

I started adding commentary to my garden games. One day I became so engrossed in a particular bit of last-minute drama as I made a last ditch attempt to evade the challenge of the rotary clothes line and get my shot away to try and complete a remarkable FA Cup semi-final comeback from a three-nil half time deficit, I was aware someone was watching me. Lost in the moment, I continued and scored the winning goal. As is always the way in these thrilling finales, there was "barely time for the opposition to restart the match…" and I breathlessly began my summing up of "one of the greatest semi-finals Villa Park had ever witnessed…".

"Wow that's brilliant" a voice from over my shoulder remarked. I spun around and saw my next door neighbour who'd only just moved in with his foot on a shovel in the ground, clapping his gloved hands. My face instantly flushed beetroot red and I quickly made for the gate back up to our flat with him still clapping and grinning as I left. His praise may have been genuine, but I couldn't help thinking he was mocking me. My innate sense of 'stranger danger' contributed to my swift exit. That innate sense would soon dessert me however.

I was keen to step up my football career. I longed to graduate from the clothes line centre backs, thorny rose-bush sidelines which had claimed so many of my Woolworths-bought footballs and those wonky inaccurate goalposts with their lop-sided 'keeper. I wanted to play in a team, with a proper kit, referee, nets in the goals, and more than anything I wanted Dad to be on the sidelines watching.

I figured that, if I could find myself a team to play for, Dad would show the same enthusiasm for watching his only son taking part in the beautiful game as he did for supporting his beloved Millwall. There were opportunities to play for my school in the coming year on Saturday mornings and local junior teams would play on Sundays. How amazing would that be? Dad watches son play football in the morning, takes him to the match in the afternoon, then watches him again on Sunday morning. I could extend that magical time with Dad threefold – although he'd have to watch his language of course.

I'm not sure why but I felt Dad was better approached with a fait accompli. I was great at hatching plans, thinking through the various processes and stages and assuming the outcome right up to the desired final result. Most of these schemes only existed in my head and were never executed. They usually involved ruses to getting my hands on certain Christmas or birthday presents. In this case it would be to find a team, get myself in and then announce to Dad when and where he had to be to watch my first game. This was my first attempt at putting one into practice and I quickly learned the valuable lesson that assumption is the mother of all fuck-ups, and it was a lesson that would lead me down a very dangerous road.

It was the start of a new term at my school in September 1980 and Ian, a friend of mine who sat a few rows behind me was excitedly telling anyone who would listen one Friday afternoon that he was going to football trials the next day. This in itself struck me as rather odd as Ian was into cricket, a game that I just did not understand, and we were often at loggerheads when discussing the merits of our own favourite sports. However, as there were very few opportunities for eight-year-olds to play team cricket in our area, Ian's dad thought it would do him good to join the local junior football team, organised by a well-known local coach by all accounts.

Trials were to take place over the next two Saturday mornings at our local rec, the team would be picked and compete during the 80-81 season in the local Croydon Junior Football League. I could barely contain my excitement; this is what I had trained for all summer long, the hours spent whacking the ball against the fence and curling volleys into the top corner of the swings was all going to pay off now.

I explained to my dad that I was going to the rec for a couple of hours with Ian and his dad, nothing more, so as not to spoil the surprise once my place in the team was secured. I took the short walk down to the bottom of my road and met Ian and his dad on the corner as agreed. I turned and waved to my dad who had taken a brief break from his duties in the front garden to make sure I was safely in the care of another adult before going back to his digging.

From years of watching my dad in the garden, the only thing I could grasp that he ever did was to plunge his spade in the mud, turn over great clumps of soil, then hack away at them, before prodding them with the fork. He'd spend almost all of his Saturday and Sunday mornings – weather permitting – avidly focussed on this bizarre, seemingly pointless and monotonous chore. It was almost impossible to talk to him while he did it, any distraction seemed to irritate him more than usual. It almost felt like this was his penance for his Saturday afternoon enjoyment which had to be earned with a few hours solid hard labour. I was convinced that I'd soon have something far better for him to spend his weekend mornings on.

As we entered the gates of South Norwood Recreation Ground we were greeted by the site of a large gathering of noisy excited boys of various ages. They were messily congregated in front of the pavilion which housed changing rooms and toilets as well as a large shelter where you could take refuge in sudden downpours. This was situated next to the main football pitch of four on the large park and separated by the path that led through it and joined its three different entrances. As we made our way toward the group which we assumed was the rest of the trial candidates I suddenly realised that this wasn't going to be the formality that I first imagined.

I quickly recognised several boys from my school in the years above me and a few that looked even older – high school age even – which to me back then was virtually adult. Footballs were being randomly kicked against the wall and other boys and every few seconds two or three would break away from the pack in a race to retrieve a ball. A handful of boys were diligently doing keepie-ups, one could only assume to try and gain the advantage of making a favourable early impression with the coach.

As we arrived at the edge of the throng to gawps from those clearly perturbed by the addition of two more extra players to compete for their places, I experienced, for the first time, that humiliating ritual of being 'sized up' as one or two of the boys looked me up and down to make an assessment of my footballing ability and therefore threat before dismissing me with a smirk. So far there was still no sign of anyone in charge of the event, just a bunch of kids. Ian's dad, the only parent present, was starting to look irritated. He was a teacher, very well-spoken, strict, but a friendly and kind man. He was always very chatty whenever I had been to Ian's house.

Suddenly a cry went up:

"Here he is, OI SPLODGEGUN!"

The shout was greeted with giggles and shushes. We turned to where the boys were looking to see two figures walking towards us from the entrance gates.

As they came into view I could make out a tall adult figure and a shorter younger male. The younger one had a football under his left arm and a large bag of balls over his right shoulder, he was moving much quicker, purposefully towards us, before stopping at the edge where the path met the grass a few feet in front of us, ceremoniously dropping the back onto the mud and then drop-kicking the ball in his hands powerfully toward one of the goals on the pitch. I guessed he was about 12 or 13 but he had features that made him appear much older. He was quite short but stocky and looked strong. He had dark thick wiry black hair and his face looked how I can only describe as rough, 'weathered'. He was the archetypal 'neighbourhood tough kid' and all the boys seemed to know him as Rob.

Rob glanced over to see that his adult companion had already arrived but wasn't quite in earshot and stepped forward to address the crowd:

"Right, stop fucking calling him Splodgegun OK? You know he hates it, his name's Derek"

Giggles broke out again and Rob appeared to be stifling laughter himself, even though his tone seemed deadly serious. I looked up at Ian's dad who looked back at me and raised an eyebrow which reminded me of Roger Moore, he didn't say anything but the look was enough to say that he didn't approve of Rob's robust approach.

Then he arrived: Spoldgegun. Derek.

His arrival had been announced not just by Rob's reminder of what to call him, but the clumping scuffling noise that he made as he dragged his feet in heavy black boots across the ground.

Standing at about six feet tall, he wore a long, heavy waterproof coat, like a trench coat. He was balding, but with long slicks of greasy black hair swept back over his head behind each ear. Then there was his face. The left side was distorted as if he was squinting in the sun but only on one side, similarly the left side of his mouth was turned up to reveal his teeth and in the permanently open left corner of his mouth a foam of spittle gathered and frothed from between his teeth.

I was unaware of it at the time but he suffered from a condition known as Bell's palsy, a type of facial paralysis that results in an inability to control the facial muscles on the affected side. This caused the spittle to gather and made for quite a display when he spoke – which is why the local children had cruelly nicknamed him splodgegun – after the foam-shooting weapons made famous by the popular child film Bugsy Malone a few years earlier. I'd only lived in the area a short time but it seemed that he and Rob were well-known on the junior football circuit. I heard rumours that Rob was part of a family of travelers who had settled in housing in the area which was quite common in south London in the seventies and eighties. Of course I never dared ask him if this was the case. Rob it seemed was Derek's right hand man, his captain.

As he addressed the assembled masses of wannabe footballers, Derek explained, through a shower of saliva and to a backdrop of more awkward, stifled giggles, how proceedings would work. The group would be assembled into a single match of eleven versus eleven, the remainder would wait on the sidelines while Derek and Rob assessed the players, swapping and subbing players as the game went on to try and get an accurate appraisal of each boy. At the end of the two-hour session, some would be asked to come back next week, the others would be dropped from the process. Eventually his team Spartan Royals, would be formed. It all seemed very well thought-out, despite the farcical start to proceedings. Ian's dad however was not convinced and, as we made our way over to the pitch to start, I saw him leading Ian towards the gate. I ran after him, asking what was wrong.

"I'm not having my son playing with THAT" he barked. By 'that' I assumed he meant Derek and I instantly felt sorry for him. Clearly his disability wasn't his fault and whilst his personal hygiene also left a little to be desired, he seemed to know what he was talking about. My usual reservations about strangers, scary-looking men or anyone that made me feel a little uneasy were cast aside. I was blinded by my desperation to play football and, if I'm honest, whilst Ian's departure meant I was literally on my own without either a friend I knew or an adult to supervise me, it also meant I had a better chance of making the team.

I assured Ian's dad that it was OK for me to stay and that my dad was coming down soon anyway, which of course was a lie, and joined the rest of the boys to stake my claim for a place in the squad. I had already missed the cut for the first 22 but was happier taking my place on the side next to six or seven other boys waiting for their chance because it gave me the opportunity to weigh up the competition. It didn't bode well. It was a real mix of ages with very few boys appearing to be as young as me and most two, three or even more years older. As the game progressed, it was dominated by Rob who was constantly barking orders to pass or shoot. Derek was offering encouragement, animatedly following the play up and down the line, moving from one foot to the next and letting out a loud "Wallaaaah" every time a shot was either saved or ended up in the goal.

After about ten minutes I decided a good tactic would be to stand close to him so I was in view and remind him to try me out when he decided to make some changes. I followed him up and down the line, making what I thought to be clever observations. After a few he looked at me and smiled. When I say smiled, it was as much a smile as his face could muster, it was more of a matching of the permanent grimace his left side presented with the right, quite terrifying really. But again, I was blinded by football in a situation that would normally have had me running for Mum and Dad.

After a while he started to talk to me, asked my name, where I lived, the usual stuff, although not what position I preferred to play which I thought odd. Then my ploy appeared to work and my chance arrived. Me and two other boys were subbed on to the disdain of those brought off. For the next twenty minutes or so I tried in vain to even get a touch of the ball. Nobody would pass to me and I was just far too weak and slow in the tackle to go and get the ball myself. I'd adopted another ploy to try and get myself noticed by Derek by staying wide and operating up and down the wing close to his gaze, but without seeing any of the ball it was a pointless exercise. Just as I was starting to accept that it wasn't to be a loose ball pinged out to me from a melee of legs in the centre circle, I controlled it and headed for goal but rushed a shot as two large boys thundered in towards me. It was first ever experience of actually being challenged in a proper football match. Our tennis ball school playground games were played with the unwritten rule that you didn't really tackle because of the consequences of hitting the tarmac, those games were more for finesse than displays of brute strength. Similarly, being chased down by two lads twice my size was a very different proposition to taking on my mum's rotary washing line in my back garden.

The ball nestled safely into the goal keeper's arms but above the hoots of derision came a loud "Walaaaah". It was Derek and he was voicing his approval of my feeble effort on goal. I was puzzled but also elated. Perhaps it hadn't looked as bad as it seemed?

Minutes later I was subbed off again and Derek rested an arm on my shoulder and said: "Well played, Mervyn, really impressive" and was far less animated as the rest of the session played out. When it was over Derek and Rob huddled together to discuss the decision-making process and then Derek walked among us tapping those who he wanted to see next week on the head. After a prodding several good footballers on the head with a thick grubby finger and barking a spittle-filled "you", he walked slowly over to me and rested his hand softly on my head and breathed the word "and you". Then I noticed Rob looking at me and as our eyes met, he smiled, signaled an exaggerated 'thumbs up' and bellowed: "Nice one our Mervyn!" in a strange, effected northern accent.

The whole situation should have unnerved me, set alarm bells ringing and filled my head with visions of those short films they used to show you in school about not believing tales of going to see some puppies. That was my usual reaction to such situations. If I was out shopping with my mum and a stranger winked or smiled at me, even if his intentions were entirely innocent and friendly I assumed he wanted to bundle me in to the back of his car and speed off. But this was different. This was football, it was all fine. Or so I thought. The main part of my plan was to make it in to the team, after that I didn't really have to have much to do with Derek apart from training and pre-match or half time team talks because I was going to be under the watchful gaze of my dad. It never occurred to me just how much I was taking for granted and the potential danger I was placing myself in, although I was to get a little hint of it for the first time quite soon.

A week later greatly reduced numbers assembled again at the rec. A lot of the boys who had been asked to return hadn't bothered and it was clear that by default I was going to at the very least make up part of a match day squad. I arrived late, having spent a little time persuading my parents I was OK to walk the short distance down to the park. You could virtually see the road that led off the high street down to the rec from just outside our front gate and I reasoned that it was no different to having the run of the estate on my own back in Balham at a younger age.

When I arrived at the rec the atmosphere was noticeably different from the previous week – and Derek had a companion with him. As I walked towards him he looked up from his conversation with his colleague and seemed pleased to see me, but in a less enthusiastic and animated way than before. He immediately introduced me to his friend whose name I didn't catch, which was already quite common in conversations with Derek. I quickly learned to make them as brief as possible to avoid the equally awkward situations of being spattered with spittle or not hearing what he'd said and, being too shy to ask him to repeat, merely nodding my head as if I got the message.

This introduction was to provide the first of Derek's tales of his links with the Football Association. Over the coming months we'd all hear these long rambling stories about how he went to meetings with local FA officials and then meetings at the actual FA headquarters, convincing us that he was a figure of authority when it came to junior football. We didn't understand or care about any of it of course. All we could hear was affiliation this and affiliation that with plenty of Lancaster Gates thrown in, and each time he mentioned Lancaster Gate he added the aside: "which is the headquarters of the Football Association", often two or three times in the same pointless incoherent speech. These sessions used to take place in the waiting room of South Croydon train station after training where Derek would wait with us all until the train arrived to take us the two stops home, but more about that later.

Derek's friend was, along with him, in some way connected with the club's affiliation to the FA, but the long-winded introduction quickly faded into the background as I made eye contact with the man. At the time my first instinct was that he looked like the child catcher in Chitty Chitty Bang Bang, if only for his long straggly hair and rodent-like eyes.

Years later, when I was sat in the cinema with my two sons watching one of the Harry Potter films I felt sick to my stomach when the character Argus Filch appeared for the first time. This was Derek's 'friend', right there in front of me. The resemblance was uncanny.

He didn't wear a hat, but, like Derek, wore a similar long coat with big pockets and gave off a distinctive and sickening smell which was a mixture of body odour and cigarette smoke. He was holding a heavy Safeways carrier bag in each hand. He seemed to glare angrily, almost right through me and, unnerved by this, I switched my gaze to what he was carrying which seemed to agitate him. I wasn't sure why he was there, but he remained for the entire session during which Derek seemed to be much more serious and less jovial than the previous week. The pair shared brief and very important-looking exchanges at various stages of the games.

At the end of the session, Derek announced that this was his team and league matches would start the following Sunday. A buzz of excitement filled the group. Meanwhile, Derek's companion was leaving. None of the players seemed to know who he was and, it appeared, none of them had been given the awkward introduction that I'd had earlier. I felt relieved to see him go, his presence made me feel for the first time that something wasn't right about all this. Derek explained that we'd meet for matches here at the rec and catch the bus to Lloyd Park in south Croydon which is where all matches would be played. I explained that I'd be going with my dad and that seemed to flick a switch in Derek.

"Ah yes, I need to speak to your parents to make sure I have their permission for you to be in the team".

I can remember those words particularly clearly, because it was such an unusually eloquent sentence, seemingly so well-rehearsed.

As the crowd dissipated, I explained that I only lived a few minutes away and Derek said it would be best to walk me home and speak to them straight away. As we made our way to my house I started to feel my earlier reservations melt away. This suddenly felt right again. I had made it into the team, the manager was decent enough to meet my parents to get their approval and introduce himself and, after all, I'd be attending all matches with Dad anyway so even if his grim companion did turn up, there'd be no repeat of the earlier unpleasantness.

As we arrived at my front gate we were greeted by both my mum and dad. Dad, who had spent his usual Saturday morning in the garden digging up dirt, was leaning up against the pebbledash bin shed drinking from a pint glass of orange squash that Mum had brought him, just as she always did when his gardening shift was coming to an end. Both of them were looking at me slightly puzzled as I arrived home with Derek huffing and puffing and clumping along just behind me. I quickly explained who he was and why he was here before he too arrived at the gate and introduced himself. He then rambled on about the team and then threw in some Football Affiliations and the mandatory Lancaster Gate. His "which by the way is where the FA Headquarters are" was met with an immediate "Yeah I know where the FA Headquarters are" from my dad who never liked to be schooled on football minutiae. As he explained the Sunday matches and

Friday evening training sessions, and how he would accompany and supervise the boys in them all, I was waiting for my dad to jump in and explain that he'd be bringing me.

The first problem here was Friday nights were out as far as Dad was concerned as this was the day he would go straight to his mum's in Peckham from work, spend the evening with her and get the train home, not getting back until after 9pm. I wasn't aware of the Friday night training, maybe I just hadn't heard in our earlier Derek debriefing, it was easy to switch off while he was frothing away.

Next, to my horror, I caught sight of my mum. Her eyes were fixed on Derek's distinctive features and she was doing nothing to hide her apparent disgust. Worse than this, her mouth was open and moving in the similar awkward angles to Derek's, mimicking him. I'm pretty sure she was doing this subconsciously, the same way some people's lips move when they are reading, but all the same the embarrassment was reddening my face almost as much as the anxiety for Dad to explain that he'd be taking me to games. The conversation ended suddenly with a handshake and a "Cheerio" and Derek clumped off down the road. Then came the post-mortem.

With a mixture of laughter and disgust, Mum absolutely slaughtered Derek for the state that he was. While I tried to defend him, saying that whatever caused the disfigurement of his face wasn't his fault, she pointed out that there was no excuse for him to dress and smell like a tramp. With that she disappeared inside. Dad meanwhile was busy putting his gardening tools away into his small shed in the back garden. This, like any tidying up task that Dad was involved in, was done with military-style precision and efficiency.

I used to marvel at the way he would spend as much time preparing and tidying away as he did on the actual task itself. It's a regime with deep roots in craftsmanship, but for Dad, I would later discover it to be a more far-reaching and personal symptom. As he completely emptied the shed of all its contents and neatly laid it out on the patio – including the shelves of jam jars and margarine or ice cream containers that now housed various bits of odd-job and DIY paraphernalia – I started to broach the subject of him taking me to football the following Sunday. I built up to it slowly, telling him about where the matches were, what time they kicked off, and what time we'd be home, before nervously getting to the big question.

I was nervous because by now his distinct lack of enthusiasm for the whole thing made me feel that this wasn't going to go the way I had planned. I partly hoped that this was because Dad was focussed on his tidying-up operation. I quickly learned that Dad wasn't happy being distracted from the focus of tidying and could be snappier than usual at times like this, so my timing wasn't great and it may have been best left until later, but eight-year-olds don't work on that kind of logic. When you're eight, everything has to be immediate, and I was right to be nervous about asking Dad to extend his footballing passion to watching me play.

"Whaaat?"

That was Dad's stock response to being asked something when he wanted to make it abundantly clear right from the start that he had no intention of entertaining it. A prolonged "What?" said so much more than simply: "I beg your pardon, would you mind repeating the question please?"

Dad was having none of it. There was no way he was giving up his Sunday to be running around all over the place on buses all day after spending the week commuting to work. Exaggeration was another Dad trick. I tried to point out that it was a fifteen minute walk to the bus stop and a further fifteen on the bus to south Croydon; a couple of hours of watching football – which he so loved to do – and then another half hour journey home. That was still a sizeable chunk out of Dad's day of rest though and I knew he wasn't budging.

What hurt me more was that in the previous years when we'd lived in Balham, a regular Sunday morning ritual would be for us to walk to the local newsagent after breakfast where dad would buy his Sunday paper and some sweets for me and we'd then take the 30 minute stroll down to Clapham Common where the vast array of football pitches were filled with games. Eventually, Dad would find one that he recognised and there, managing from the side lines would be George, a chubby, ruddy-faced, smiley character who had run men's football teams for pretty much most of his adult life. Dad had played for two of his teams, one of them particularly good apparently. They were called Holderness United and in the seasons that Dad had been there they had enjoyed footballing trips to Holland and Belgium. We would watch the match and Dad would chat with George and the players he knew. George would laugh and chat with me, ruffling my hair and handing me sections of orange from the bag of half-time refreshments. It introduced me to another side of football and was part of what made me so keen to play myself. I loved Dad's stories of the camaraderie of his playing days and could tell he missed it, so it made me all the more puzzled as to why he wanted nothing to do with me playing the game he loved so much.

Our discussion turned into a row. Well, as close to a row as you can have with your dad when you're eight, it was a tantrum from me interspersed with increasingly loud shouting from Dad. This put him in a foul mood for the rest of the day, foul enough for him to refuse to go to the day's Millwall home match. I was mortified. In trying to strengthen my bond with my dad I felt like I had broken it.

I was a stubborn little bugger and for the next six months I packed my freshly-dubbined boots and shin pads and left our flat at 9:45 each Sunday morning to meet the team at the rec. Derek was never there as he said he would be, it was all organised by Rob. From there we walked to the bus stop and leapt off the open back of the big red Routemaster service just before it reached its stop for Lloyd Park. For six months those boots and shin pads were completely redundant. I spent every game at the touchline watching, with Derek regularly walking up to me and promising he'd "send me on in a minute", he was just waiting for the right time apparently. After the match we'd all bundle back on the bus and jump off a various stops. I'd make it home just in time for Sunday lunch.

Looking back I'm dumbfounded to imagine the eight-year-old me wandering the streets of south London for most of every Sunday morning. Initially I felt Dad would have a change of heart and start to come, if only to safeguard me, but both he and Mum seemed perfectly happy with the arrangement and they simply continued their little Sunday morning lives. As time went on I gave up hope of Dad getting involved and, despite the total lack of game time, started to enjoy a similar camaraderie that I saw my dad enjoy as I befriended the small number of other non-playing subs that travelled to every game.

As the season drew to a close, Derek gathered us all together at the final whistle of the last match. He had at his feet a large bin bag which clinked as he carefully rested it on the floor. Boys around me nudged each other excitedly as if they knew what was coming. I had no idea. Derek gave a speech, the usual Football Association Lancaster Gate waffle and then proceeded to call out each player's name and as they came forward to rounds of applause from their teammates, he shook their hand and then stooped down and grabbed something out of the bag.

He handed them a wooden plaque with a shiny gold-coloured metal plate on the bottom and a shiny plastic image of a footballer in the middle, then he handed them a small silver coloured medal. I was in awe, but also disappointed. The names being called out were the boys who played week in week out and when Rob's name was called to loud cheers, I assumed that, as captain, his was the final award in the ceremony. Then he turned to me, winked and beckoned me forward. "Here you go Mervyn" he smiled, and handed me a plaque and a medal before shaking my other hand and patting me on the head. I was aware of some giggles among the rest of the team and a palpable feeling of "What is HE getting a medal for" but the awkwardness was broken by Rob shouting "Well done our Mervyn" and leading the rest of the crowd to a reluctant round of applause.

Rob had been kind to me all season. The faux-northern 'our Mervyn' thing stuck from that first day of trials. Some of the boys were fascinated with what they thought was a weird name and insisted on saying it in funny accents. It didn't bother me, it was harmless good-spirited stuff and helped me to be part of the group even though I wasn't playing. I found it strange but heartening that Rob was always chatting to me, asking if I was OK and stepping in if some of the other boys' teasing overstepped the mark.

I gleefully showed my parents my awards when I arrived home and, for a glorious few minutes, Dad showed an interest.

"It's like mine" he said as he inspected the plaque. The gold plate which was supposed to hold some sort of inscription was blank. The 'wood' backing was actually very light plastic and you could tell that both the stuck-on plastic picture of a footballer in shooting pose and blank inscription plate could slip loose at any time. He reached over to the back of the shelves in the alcove of our lounge which was home to all of our knick-knacks. Mostly Mum's, these ranged from various souvenir picture frames or novelty egg-timers from holidays; a variety of ash trays – even though no-one in my house had ever smoked, a small wooden money box with a clumsily painted picture of an old-fashioned telephone on it - apparently for when visitors use the phone to the full set of The Children's Encyclopedia on the bottom shelf.

Dad retrieved a small shield-shaped object and passed it to me. It was heavy, real wood and had a small silver plate which was screwed in place at the bottom. "Holderness United First Team 1965-66" was etched into the metal. It sat below an equally impressive image of a footballer controlling a ball with the backdrop of a stadium beautifully illustrated in great detail. Dad placed my plaque on the shelf and put his alongside it. He then inspected the medal, bringing it close to his eyes and squinting as he lifted his spectacles onto his forehead, almost like some kind of jewelry expert. He flipped it over and studied it again before gently leaning it up against my plaque. For a moment, just a few magical seconds, Dad got involved with my own football world. Then he went back to his paper and completely zoned out once more.

The whole medal award ceremony – as incongruous as it was in its muddy pitch-side setting with bin-bag and uninscribed gongs – had made up my mind to stick with football, and indeed with Spartan Royals and Derek. His scary friend had not made any more appearances and perhaps next season I would be able to work my way into the team with my first year under my belt.

With matches finished, there was still a few weeks of the regular football season left and Friday evening training sessions at Lloyd Park continued. At first these were enjoyable affairs. Small-sided games were organised and all-comers were welcomed. Some younger players had turned up and Derek organised two or three matches geared more towards even age groups which I started to do well in. I was even more encouraged when Dave, one of my best friends from school turned up and started to train with us. I was enjoying playing football on mild Spring Friday evenings with my friends. It was perfect. Or so I thought.

The evening bus service from Lloyd Park was sporadic and unreliable. Derek, in his apparent duty of care for his team, insisted on escorting all boys to the local train station and sitting with them in the waiting room until the train arrived to take them home. The talk was always of football, we'd chatter excitedly about all aspects of the game, our favourite players of the time and Derek always seemed to 'know' someone connected with the game. A young Crystal Palace starlet, a referee, every week there was a tale from Derek about how their football career had either started at Spartan Royals or been enhanced by their association with it. One Friday Derek didn't wait with us for the train to arrive.

As we walked to the station after a training session one evening, our group came to a stop at the entrance to the station. Rob asked if anyone fancied a sleepover. This was completely out of the blue but he quickly explained that, as Derek lived close to the station, they often had big sleepovers at his place. Rob made it clear that he was always there along with loads of the lads and it was a great laugh. There would be fish and chips to eat, games to play and you could phone your parents to let them know where you were as soon as you arrived.

I wasn't as suspicious of this as I should have been. It actually sounded like fun. It's just that I wasn't a sleepover kid. I'd had one attempt at staying at my friend Paul's house a few months earlier and it had been a nightmare. It was only a few miles away but the moment bedtime came and I changed into my pyjamas I felt homesick and Paul's dad had to drive me home.

As soon as there appeared to be a few boys interested in this, Derek set off with instructions to follow him. He continued past the station entrance and on to a footbridge that led over the railway. I followed on. I'm not sure why, there was no way I was sleeping over, but I was curious and as everyone else seemed to follow, including those who hadn't voiced an interest in the sleepover I didn't fancy being left at the station alone.

As we reached the other side of the footbridge we found ourselves in a cul-de-sac.

"Derek lives just down there, come on" Rob shouted as he pointed down the road that led away from the footbridge entrance. Derek was already making his way down the road with Rob hustling the three or four boys who had decided to take up the offer like a sheepdog, chivvying them along in Derek's wake. One of them was Dave. We returned to the station and took our train home.

I sat next to Dave at the front of my class. When I started the school it was midway through the first year of the juniors and being the new kid can be tough. The previous term the child who had sat next to Dave had left and I was directed to fill his seat. Me and Dave hit it off immediately, both being football and music mad. He was a fantastic footballer. He was very small. Every class has one child that is smaller than the other children don't they? Dave's diminutive stature gave him a great low centre of gravity which lent itself perfectly to his skillful dribbling and he also possessed a fearsome shot which belied his tiny build. We dominated our PE lesson matches, the only time you were allowed a regulation football in school games. Playtime football was strictly tennis ball only, but in PE we were allowed a green plastic ball, slightly heavier than the Woolworths flyaways. The teacher would often leave us to play after picking sides. Me and Dave would always manage to fix it so that we were on the same side and share the goals in the latest slaughter, something that was cottoned onto one lesson when the teacher insisted we both be captains which resulted in probably the only 0-0 draw ever to be played out in Mrs Brenchley's 1980-81 PE lessons.

Monday mornings would be filled with chatter between me and Dave, about my trip to Millwall, the latest single by The Jam, his visits to see his dad (his parents, like most of my friends, were separated or divorced) or just the usual inane stuff that pals like to exchange. Monday was the first opportunity to digest a weekend of stuff, you would never have considered phoning your friends on Saturday or Sunday for a chat or an update.

On this particular Monday morning I was keen to find out what the Derek sleepover had been like in addition to everything else, but I was met with a wall of silence. Despite me gently quizzing him throughout the day, Dave refused to talk about it. In fact, for the rest of the week he remained virtually silent. He had an older brother, also at our school, two years above us. At break time, Dave would often chat to his brother and his friends. It was something I was quite envious of and the only thing that ever made me reconsider my satisfaction with being an only child, although by virtue of being his best mate, I also gained associate membership of this exclusive little inner circle. Dave's brother and all his friends were also football-mad and allowed us to join their lunchtime matches, which was high honour indeed. On that Monday however, the regular lunchtime game appeared to have been curtailed.

Dave was clearly in deep conversation with his brother and friends and when I approached them it was made quite clear to me that I wasn't to be party to their serious-looking conference. As I was ushered away I just caught Dave's brother remarking:

"If I see him again I'm gonna kill him".

To me these boys were virtually adults. Fourth year juniors when you're a second year are big men. In the real world of course they are ten and eleven year old children, but hearing that, spoken with the venom it was, made me realise something bad had happened, and I knew it had to have something to do with Derek and the sleepover. Dave never spoke of it again, I never asked him and, needless to say, he never attended another Friday night football session. I could sense danger again, the way I had sensed it when I was introduced to Derek's friend. Then it had subsided and for the entire football season, as bizarre as it had been, with me constantly attending matches and training sessions without so much as a hint of playing any competitive football, I never felt that anything was untoward. The trophy award had cemented my faith in the whole thing being totally above board and that it was just a matter of time before I was a regular in Derek's team. Now, however, my mind was starting to unravel things in the clumsy and confused way that eight-year-old minds do. My love of football, and growing confidence which had been boosted by the acceptance of my teammates, the friendship and apparent faith shown in me by Rob, who clearly had a big influence in Derek's management, meant that I persuaded myself not to walk away, but to proceed with caution.

After the next Friday evening training session there was no talk of sleepovers, and I wasn't about to raise the matter as we took our seats in the waiting room on South Croydon station. Derek, as usual, held court. He was sat directly opposite me and each time we made eye contact I felt my head instinctively twitch away to divert his gaze. It had been a bright sunny late April day and warm playing in the evening but now, as it began to get dark, it was chilly and we were grateful for the little heater that glowed away against the wall in front of us. Derek started to talk about the up-coming FA Cup final. Tottenham were playing Manchester City and it was a highly anticipated match. In a time dominated by Liverpool, Spurs were a breath of fresh air playing with an exciting style and flair thanks to their Argentinian imports Ossie Ardiles and Ricky Villa. A buzz filled the room as we discussed how Tottenham were going to tear a struggling Manchester City apart. Then Derek started his usual routine, only this time with a twist. Once the room fell silent, he started to explain that, every year, the Football Association use a junior football team to select the mascots for the FA Cup final, and this year they had asked him. I have to keep reminding myself just how gullible I was back then as an eight-year-old because every time I think about that statement over the years I find it more and more ridiculous and unbelievable. The thing is, Derek had skillfully laid the groundwork throughout the season with his constant talk of his links with the FA. Fascinated and excited at the prospect that two of our number would be walking out with the teams at Wembley in a few weeks' time, we started to probe. Who were the lucky two boys? Derek shook his head. Had he not chosen them yet? Derek smiled; we took this to mean that he had. Were they in this room right now? Derek slowly nodded and held up one of his thick grubby fingers.

"One of them is". The buzz in the room was amplified, and you could tell Derek was loving it.

Things had certainly progressed, from refusing to tell us he had, now allowed us to narrow it down to one out of the six or seven boys that were sat in the waiting room in a matter of minutes. Completely taken in, I challenged him to name a name:

"Come on Derek, tell us". He smiled and nodded in my direction.

"Me?" I exclaimed. I was shocked at first, elated for a second and then I felt my stomach start to churn.

As the other boys in the room voiced their disdain and disapproval of the fact that I had been chosen, I couldn't avoid pressing Derek further:

"Which team, do you know? Is it Man City?"

Derek shook his head. Of course, given the option, even if you didn't support them, you'd want to be Spurs' mascot. There were gasps from a few of the other boys in the room, then silence. In the distance we could make out the unmistakable sound of a train approaching the station. Our train. I could feel the dull, aching feeling in my stomach start to build, up through my chest and seep into my legs, and yet still I pushed:

"So I'm going to be Spurs' mascot at the FA Cup final?"

Derek slowly nodded his head, with a sickly, spittle-filled grin that completed the journey of the nausea that was quickly coursing through my body into my fingertips and toes.

Derek's gaze was fixed firmly on me, and then through me, and I felt the same feeling of inescapable evil that I had only experienced once before – when he had introduced me to his friend at the start of that football season. I was frozen for what felt like hours, I felt panicked, trapped, and claustrophobic. Derek was still leering at me, the side of his face was illuminated by the glow of the fire as the dimly lit room had grown darker in the short time we had been sat there.

It felt like I was living a real-life nightmare. I was snapped out of it by the clatter of a train arriving at the platform outside. For a split second I tried to move but felt my feet glued to the spot. I wrenched myself up from my seat and ran to the door, flung it open and sprinted to the front of the now slowing train, eager to board as far away from that waiting room and Derek as I could. I twisted the handle of the train door and noticed my hand was shaking wildly. Throwing my bag onto the seat I slammed the door shut and wrestled with the metal top of the window which had to be pressed in before you could lower it. I yanked the window down and leant out, ensuring that Derek was still on the platform and hadn't boarded our train.

The small group of boys were climbing onto the carriage back down the platform outside the waiting room and Derek was shuffling away towards the exit, but my eyes remained firmly fixed on him until the train eventually jolted to a start and rumbled out of the station. I looked down the carriage and it appeared I was the only one in it. Not convinced, I ran up and down the central corridor several times to check. These were the type of trains that didn't have interconnecting carriages so once I was totally assured that I was alone I slumped breathlessly into the seat, my heart pounding noisily and hands still shaking. Minutes later the train screeched to a stop at my station and before it had come to a complete standstill I flung the door open and sprinted for the exit and then the entire half mile straight route from Norwood Junction station to my house.

Slamming the porch door behind me I rang the bell constantly, continuing to press the button even after the light had come on in the communal hallway behind the front door. I was greeted by a perplexed Mum who demanded to know what the fuss was all about. I grabbed her, wrapping my arms around her and pressing my face into her flour-dusted apron, deeply inhaling and reveling in the relief in the familiarity of her scent and something as mundane but so reassuring as a dusting of self-raising which was now on my nose, cheeks and lips. Moments later we were joined by Dad, arriving home from his regular Friday evening visit to my nan's and looking equally puzzled as to why we were both stood in the porch. For the rest of the evening neither of them were able to prize out of me what was wrong or what had happened.

I couldn't tell them what had happened, mainly because nothing had actually happened!

I wrestled with the events – or apparent non-events - of the previous seven days. Had I allowed my imagination to run away with me? How could I explain what happened with Dave? What *did* happen with Dave? Something did, but it looked as though I'd never find out. The final penny dropping for me though was the cup final mascot story. This, I had convinced myself, with good reason, aside from being an outrageous lie, was a ruse designed to entice me to a future sleepover. There would, I felt, almost certainly be some reason or other for me to visit Derek's house in order to fulfil the promise of leading out the Tottenham team at that season's FA Cup final. That night I lay in bed turning everything over and over in my head. I found it impossible to close my eyes because every time I did I could see Derek leering at me from across that waiting room. I should have felt total relief at being safe, but somehow I couldn't get that sickly feeling of impending peril out of my gut. I vowed never to play football again, then as the enormity of that promise sunk in, resolved never to go near the rec, Lloyd Park, South Croydon train station or any form of football outside the sanctuary of the school gates or my back garden again. Gradually, as the night passed and I convinced myself out loud that everything would be OK and Derek wouldn't be lurking on every street corner that I turned alone, I felt my eyes grow heavy and as they flickered shut and I felt the semi-conscious relief of no longer seeing Derek's distorted features gurning at me, I was briefly awoken again by the realisation that, in my panic, I'd left the carrier bag containing my first ever pair of football boots on the train. At first I felt annoyed, then glad. It was closure. I couldn't have looked at those boots again without thinking of that evening and Derek. Even now, if I conjure up the image of those black moulded-sole boots with the bright yellow flash down the side which my mum had bought for me at a stall on Hildreth Street Market in Balham just a year or so before, I still feel that terrifying fear in the pit of my stomach that I felt when Derek nodded towards me in that station waiting room.

I sat watching the FA Cup final with my dad a few weeks later. As the teams took to the field and the camera focused on them and the mascots, it came as no surprise that I didn't recognise either of them as being my Spartan Royals teammates. I never saw Derek again, but his legend was far-reaching. When I started high school two years later everyone knew of 'Splodgegun' it seemed, even boys who live in Upper Norwood and Crystal Palace close to where my school was and many miles further on from his usual stomping ground. Little did I know that there was possibly one last encounter left to face.

6
SOUTH YORKSHIRE FOOTBALL THERAPY

By 1987, my junior football career was nearing its end. That I'd survived that far was a miracle in itself. There wasn't a single time that I didn't think back with a shudder to those Splodgegun days every time I put on my football boots for my latest Sunday morning match with whichever team I was turning out for. I'd had a lucky escape, but wouldn't find out until much later on just how lucky it may have been. I loved playing football, but my enthusiasm for watching it had quickly taken over. I knew of loads of boys who played for our school team on Saturday mornings, another team Saturday afternoon and then again on Sunday but never visited a match throughout the whole season. Others preferred to just follow their team home and away. Very few managed both and for me it was starting to become a bit of an unnecessary burden. Right now, watching Millwall was all that mattered and I virtually sleep-walked through my first Croydon Junior Sunday League game the day after the trip to Leicester and the only thing on my mind was our next match at home to Birmingham on the following Tuesday evening.

There's something about watching football under floodlights that seems to amplify the atmosphere. Night games at The Den were always special. The narrow menacing streets which were intimidating enough in pleasant sunshine, must have been horrible for visiting fans at night. One minute you're in the middle of the bright lights and hustle and bustle of the country's capital city, the next you appear to have been transported to a land that time forgot, a malevolent concrete swampland lined with cemetery-like scrapyards casting eerie shadows across ever-narrowing streets that lead you to The Den. Us Millwall fans love it. They are the same cosy streets that hugged and protected our beloved little Den, but you'd like to think that if the Millwall crowd was worth the clichéd 'goal head start', and the less-than-salubrious surroundings were enough to knock the opposition fans and players off their game, that advantage could be cranked up a peg or two at night. Birmingham it could be argued was Millwall's first big test with two wins and a draw from their first three games. No team was really an out and out promotion favourite, just the usual sleeping giants who most assumed would, sooner or later, regain their place in the top flight, so places were very much being jostled for in one of the most open divisions in many years and Brum were considered a good early bet to go up.

The atmosphere was electric as the match kicked off with Birmingham's large following adding to the mix. If there's one way to silence a raucous Den crowd it's with an early goal and that's what happened when Tony Rees gave the visitors a fourth minute lead after a mistake by Millwall's young stand-in full back Sean Sparham. Frustration seeps from the terraces onto the pitch far quicker at Millwall than most other clubs and there was a distinct air of "Oh, here we go again" for fifteen minutes that followed the goal as Birmingham sensed that the home fans had already turned on their team. Mercifully George Lawrence's equaliser before half time revitalised the crowd but Birmingham dug in and as the match entered the final ten minutes it was looking like two more points lost.

The roar that greeted Millwall's second goal is a sensation that I can still recall today. I've been in far bigger crowds, at far more important Millwall matches since that night, and yet I still can't remember a louder explosion of delight coupled with palpable relief as defender Alan Walker gleefully trickled the ball into an empty net after a parried shot. You would have thought that promotion itself had been clinched with that goal, when all it really did was keep alive the illusion that we were witnessing a team going all out for promotion.

Deep down none of us really believed it would last more than a couple of months, but just as you cling to the myth of Santa ever more tentatively with each passing Christmas growing up until you finally give in to the reality, we were prepared to believe that, as long as we were winning and there were enough points to play for, there was a chance we'd somehow achieve the impossible.

When Keith 'Rhino' Stevens – another defender – crashed home a third in the last minute, it was greeted by another huge roar that belied the 6,000 crowd and, we hoped, would send out a message to the other promotion hopefuls as well as sending us up from eleventh to fourth in the table.

When you're faced with unexpected success as a football fan, no matter how short-lived or trivial, it can do strange things to you. Fourth place in Division Two was the stuff of dreams for me. Even though the season was barely three weeks old, I couldn't wait to see the league tables on Teletext updated that night. After checking several times and seeing that they hadn't been changed, I clicked again at about 10:30pm and saw that they had been updated but, to my horror, INCORRECTLY!

There was Millwall with a record to place them in fourth spot, but inexplicably back in seventh, even though their points total was better than the two teams above them. Apoplectic, I dialled directory enquiries and demanded to know the phone number for Oracle and then set about calling to complain. After being put through to about four different departments, I finally got to speak to a very tired-sounding chap who confirmed he worked in the sport department. After explaining my problem with their football table faux pas to a backdrop of audible impatient sighs from the other end of the line, I finished my rant and waited for him to respond.

"Look, there's only two of us working here you know…"

At which point the completely ridiculous folly of my Basil Fawlty-style complaint hit me. I carefully replaced the receiver and went to bed.

Perspective, which I had clearly lost quite dramatically with my meltdown over a league table four games into the season, is a very rare commodity among football fans. Whilst the game follows form for most of the time, the mad chaos of it where anyone is capable of beating anyone is the magic that sustains its popularity.

The second Millwall match that my dad took me to was a home game against Exeter in 1979. By half time we were 5-0 up.

"They'll get another five in the second half" quipped a fellow fan as he passed us on the terraces on his way for a half time, tea, beer or toilet break. My dad laughed and agreed. For me it was a given. Surely if we were good enough to score five in 45 minutes a 10-0 final score line was the least we could expect? The match finished 5-1 and I can even remember a few boos at the final whistle. I was immediately perplexed, fascinated and hooked all at the same time. A few weeks later we played struggling Mansfield at home. On discovering that they had been beaten 2-1 by Exeter earlier in the season I couldn't wait to watch the slaughter unfold at The Den. The game finished 2-2.

That is of course is an illustration of the extreme naivety of a seven-year-old whose world is still very much black and white. The trouble is there are fully grown adults who still hold faith in the same simple logic. They are football fans. For many the game contains a few simple equations: we lose: we're shit, we lose again, the manager's shit; we win: we're going up etc., and so from one week to the next during the football season we abandon all reasoning skills and instead let our emotions take the wheel.

The Saturday after we had achieved what we considered a hard-earned win against a decent Birmingham side likely to be challenging us for a top two spot at the end of the season, two results put us firmly in our place. Millwall's 1-3 submission away to Bradford was hard enough to take, but it was the result that preceded it in the final scores that day which gave us something to think about: Birmingham City 0, Crystal Palace 6

The Second Division promotion race was starting to resemble the start of the Grand National or the opening of the doors on sales day. Almost every team it seemed fancied their chances of going up and far from being a front-runner with our legion of new signings, we seemed to be heading for the most expensive season of mid-table mediocrity in the club's history.

The atmosphere for the next home game against Ipswich was resigned. It was only September and no team had ever won any honours while the leaves were still on the trees, but for Millwall fans weary from decades of false hope, it was all too familiar.

As the game ticked through its final ten minutes with the teams locked at 1-1, even the award of a late penalty for Millwall didn't seem to rouse the crowd that much. It was however a nice moment to savour watching Kevin O'Callaghan ruthlessly despatch the spot kick for his first Millwall goal since returning to the club where it had all started against the team he left us for.

"A Kevin O'Callaghan penalty". Remember those words, they figure quite a lot later on.

Determined to keep the faith, I bought two away travel tickets for the following Saturday's trip to Sheffield United during the half time break. Steve wasn't able to go and a few other friends I asked weren't keen and so another plot was hatched to make sure I made the trip, although it didn't go exactly to plan.

Before that, we had a midweek visit to Manchester City. Freshly relegated, but without a win since the opening day, they were struggling and this would surely be our first away win to nicely set up my trip to Sheffield United who were also languishing at the wrong end of the table.

Wednesday was full school assembly day at school. The 1100 or so incumbents of Sylvan High School would file reluctantly into the huge, grey breeze blocked sports hall, ushered in by beleaguered teachers, and sit cross-legged on the dusty floor with its flaking multi-coloured stick-on lines marking out the various sports that it hosted. Chatting was 'shushed' and every slap, yelp, fart and giggle resounded around the dismal chasm. On the signal from the deputy head, who had to use a microphone to ensure his voice wasn't lost in space, we'd all stand again while the headmaster strode purposefully in through the doors and made his way to the front, taking the microphone from his number two and asking us to sit. Cue more fuss, fighting and admonishment from weary teachers dreaming of when they'd be back in the staff room again.

"Sit down", "stand up", "sit down". If you want a recipe for juvenile anarchy, it's a good place to start.

There would then follow a long drawn out story about some bloke or other from some place or other who did something or other leading to a deep meaningful moral that we should all pay attention to lest we befall the same fate.

Then, before handing back to the deputy to go through all the various school sporting results, he asked us to "spend a few minutes contemplating or praying – according to our beliefs – about how we can learn from today's story". I attended that school and most of its full school assemblies from September 1983 until May 1988 and I'm 100% certain that not one single pupil took the head up on that offer. Apart from one that is.

These minutes of contemplation were usually spent looking around, seeing if anyone was doing anything that remotely resembled praying and marking their card ready for break-time ridicule and a good kicking, so the golden rule was to adopt a pose that avoided any chance of this. I certainly wasn't a believer by any stretch of the imagination, so what I did next was completely spontaneous, out of sheer desperation and at the risk of total humiliation: I prayed for Millwall to win at Manchester City that night.

Obviously I didn't do the whole hands together looking to the heavens thing – for the exact reason mentioned above, but in the instant we were asked to get praying, I thought: "Sod it, what have I got to lose? You never know, it might just work…"

So whilst affecting the "Oh I really can't be arsed with this, I had such a late night last night I can barely keep me eyes open" stance, I muttered – in my head of course - a clumsily composed invocation that involved something along the lines of promising to visit church more often and taking the big guy more seriously in future if he could just see his way clear to guiding The Lions to three points on their travels that evening.

I spent the rest of the school day relieved that I hadn't been rumbled and increasingly convincing myself that this ridiculous ruse might just hold water. Maybe, I thought, this is why religious folk are so upbeat about the whole God thing, the power of prayer and all that. Don't knock it until you've tried it eh?

Football fans are hopeless dreamers, and fifteen-year-olds, whilst long past the tooth fairy and Easter bunny stage, haven't completely lost all of their faith in some sort of magic. A combination of the two is catastrophic.

I decided to avoid the match by shutting myself away in my room. Dad had strict instructions not to interrupt me with updates. I lay on my bed, the time passing excruciatingly slowly while I let Docherty's men work God's will. I gave it until nine thirty and decided to venture downstairs. Dad was in his usual chair as I entered the front room and as soon as I entered he turned to me and rolled his eyes.

That could mean anything coming from my dad, good or bad, it was the facial expression that followed the eye-rolling that told the story. I've seen him roll his eyes reveling in a big win or reeling from news of a crushing defeat. I didn't need to wait long for the verdict, delivered in typically level-headed fashion:

"Four nil. FOUR." He repeated the "four" loudly and with extra emphasis, in a similar way that the vidiprinter spells out large scores in brackets on the television to reinforce their extreme nature and confirm they are genuine and not the result of some errant, ham-fisted typist.

"I tell you what, they'll be going down this season never mind up, they need to sack that Docherty, he's useless. Cascarino's a waste of money too, Sheringham's stopped scoring since we signed him…" his rant continued. It was the sort of over-reaction and exaggeration I had grown accustomed to and Dad had it down to a fine art, always ready to condemn each and every player the moment the final whistle sounded, threatening never to go again, and then in the cold light of day realising he couldn't possibly carry out such an outrageous threat.

It's the reason Sky Sports like to grab the manager as soon as the match finishes. That is obviously when you can capture a defeated coach at his rawest and most vulnerable and get your best soundbites, and the scathing barbs about the officiating that will have him fined which, in the old days of having to wait until he'd spent some time debriefing his team and begging his chairman for one last chance, wouldn't have happened anywhere near as often as they do these days. It's the same for the players – although mercifully it's usually only the victorious ones that have the microphone thrust under their noses before they have chance to get their first post-match glug of Gatorade. But even then, you can still hear controversial comments from players that are sometimes enough to get them in hot water, make the back page headlines in the following morning's papers or, more likely these days, go viral on social media.

Dad's words tailed off as he left the room and headed upstairs to the bathroom and I clicked confirmation of the mauling on teletext, ignoring the protests of my mum, angered at having her evening television viewing interrupted.We'd been thrashed. It couldn't have gone any worse. From upstairs a voice could still be heard from behind the bathroom door:

".. and that Horne is no good either, he's too small for a goalkeeper, he's a bleedin' midget…"

Somehow I had to explain to my irate dad that he'd be accompanying me to Sheffield on Saturday.

My spiritual experiment had been an abject failure. That was me and religion finished.

I had told Dad earlier that week that I was travelling to Sheffield United with a Millwall-supporting friend from school. He still wasn't keen on me travelling so far but accepted that I was old enough to go to long distance away games, especially as I'd managed to make it to Leicester and back "without getting myself murdered" as long as I was with someone. They didn't have to be older than me anymore. The shackles were quickly being released. It seems a bit over-the-top now, but without mobile phones to keep tabs on your offspring, you can understand why he was perhaps a little bit more protective than he needed to be. Besides which, if anything did happen to me, the blame from my mum would lay squarely with him for getting me hooked on following Millwall in the first place.

Of course my friend wasn't going at all. I knew when I told my dad I'd been let down, he'd take up the spare ticket and come with me – albeit reluctantly. The plan was to leave it as late as possible so there was no chance of asking anyone else. A win at Manchester City would've helped oil the wheels a little, so the 4-0 thumping we received 48 hours before I dropped the bombshell didn't help.

Neither did the fact that Dad was suffering from a stinking cold. Knocking back the Night Nurse, he was just about to take to his bed anticipating a weekend of rehabilitation when I explained that I'd been let down by my travelling companion. The negotiation process to get from that point to him angrily agreeing to come with me took about an hour, after I rebuffed suggestions of asking anyone else, getting a refund (no chance) and him paying me for the tickets.

Deep down my old man was a softie. He secretly loved the fact that I was so keen to follow his beloved Lions all over the country and, I guessed, a little envious of my freedom to be able to just buy a ticket and jump on a train without any earache – which he would have got from my mum had he made a habit of following Millwall home and away.

So, as the football special juddered out of Kings Cross the following morning, I knew that his furious face belied the pride within. Even when, twenty minutes into the journey the heating on the antiquated old carriage spluttered to a halt leaving us freezing for the remainder of the journey to south Yorkshire, I reasoned that the tutting and shaking of his head, mouthing the words "This is fucking ridiculous…" was just a front. I hoped with all my heart that it would all be worth it.

The weather didn't improve and it was one of those days where it just rained hard and steady all day without any hope of letting up. We huddled on the away terrace and there were brief glimpses of enthusiasm from my dad as the few hundred or so hardy souls that had joined us made themselves heard. Twenty minutes in and a quick ball forward from Millwall defender Steve Wood found winger David Byrne who eluded his marker and poked a hopeful toe at the ball, diverting it into the net over the 'keeper. From our vantage point at the opposite end of the stadium, through a fug of muddy Yorkshire drizzle, it was hard to make out anything more than the unmistakable ripple of white net as ball nestled satisfyingly within.

Footballers say that scoring a goal is the best feeling in the world. Seeing your team score can't be that far behind. Seeing them take the lead after spending hours on a freezing cold train and being slowly escorted to the ground in the pissing rain whilst being stared at by the locals as if you are mass murderers being led to the gallows must be the fan equivalent of that ultimate euphoria that players experience when the ball hits the back of the net. It's a few moments of magic that justify dozens of fruitless, goalless trips every season, only topped by a last minute winner.

Then of course comes the real ordeal – waiting for the final whistle. Once it becomes clear that there's little chance of your team adding to their score and actually allowing you to enjoy the experience, the madness starts. Your perception of events on the pitch becomes completely distorted. I'm certain that, to Sheffield United fans, we looked perfectly comfortable and the game had 0-1 written all over it. From where we were standing, the home team seemed to be edging toward the inevitable equaliser – and then of course winning goal – with every attack. You lose all sense of time. It feels like the second half has been played for several hours, while yet another check of the watch shows that it's barely half way through.

Then the goal comes.

Again, it's scored at the opposite end and we see little more than a bunch of different coloured shirted bodies and a white blur as the ball pings around the penalty box following a corner and then the ripple – a far more sickening sight this time – of the net bulging.

The flipside to seeing your team score away is of course the moment the home side do the same. There seems to be an odd split-second gap of silence between the moment you realise they've scored, and the fans erupting into sound, but then it builds quickly to an echoing roar that surrounds you, compounding your misery. Millwall fans have a unique response to conceding a goal. It's called 'The Monks Chant'. It's a unique, tribal, almost eerie and foreboding sound that is basically the first syllable of 'Millwall' sung at a menacingly low pitch. It's something that, in the world of terrace chants which are plagiarised and adapted to suit various teams, has remained totally unique to Millwall.

So whilst the home fans celebrate either side of us, the one thing you shouldn't do is look at them. That would be stupid, it would only rub it in. Human nature however forces us to do the one thing our common sense advises us against and you find yourself looking across to the adjacent stand and at the fans waving at you, gesticulating, laughing. It feels like they're actually making eye contact with you personally. So we quickly get all the various curses off our chests that instinctively follow, take a deep breath and give out a loud "MMMMMMMIIIIIIIIIIIIIIIIIIIIIIIII"

To us, it sounds as if our defiant roar has drowned out the home fans' celebrations. It hasn't of course, but it beats standing there looking down at your shoes.

The goal came with about twenty minutes left and the inevitable expectation amongst most of us was for the misery to be completed with another goal – most likely with the last kick of the game. The wave of attacks continued for about ten minutes, fueled mostly by the energy generated by the heightened atmosphere and expectation that the goal has created, then fizzled out. Both teams seem to have called a truce. Home fans start to trickle away and announcements are made about away fans being kept in after the final whistle, the man of the match, attendance, next home game etc, and you wonder if the players, on hearing this, assume it to be an indirect instruction to wind it down for the day.

Then it comes, literally from nowhere.

The ball pings around the midfield with no-one able to control it, until Cascarino manages to lay the ball a short distance back to Hurlock who has seen O'Callaghan on the edge of the centre circle, marshalled by a single defender. The ball bounces kindly onto his trusty left foot allowing him one touch which takes the defender out of the equation and leaves him on the edge of the D with the goalkeeper advancing, panic-stricken, but too late. With his second touch he coolly dispatches a low shot into the right hand corner of the net and continues his run unchecked behind the goal with both arms aloft to greet the delirious away supporters.

Our view from behind the goal, obscured by the perimeter fence and net, was almost like looking down the barrel of O'Callaghan's perfectly-fired gun. I should mention that the reason I'm able to add so much detail is that, thanks to the wonder of YouTube, the fuzzy highlights of this and many other matches are preserved for posterity online, but the final glorious seconds of that goal are preserved in my memory with perfect Ultra HD clarity and Dolby surround sound.

There are few more ridiculous sights than a group of grown men jumping around and spontaneously hugging to celebrate a late winning goal away from home. Now it's our turn to look towards the home fans. The hundreds streaming out of the exits and handful of others gesticulating angrily towards us only adds to the glee. The torturous wait for the final whistle is just another of the ordeals that you learn to endure following your team away from home. As a relative newcomer to this sadistic art, I'd soon experience the full gamut of last minute emotions.

When full time finally arrived, the ritual of players applauding fans was indulged in with almost as much gusto as the winning goal itself and, as I turned to my dad, I was relieved to see his bright red nose, sore from wiping since he'd unwillingly been dragged from his warm bed some ten hours earlier, had been joined by a ruddy set of cheeks, warm with joy on his grinning face.

Leaving the shelter of the away terrace, our damp clothes were given a fresh soaking as our Police escort took us through the dim local streets. After about 40 minutes, grumbles of how much longer it was taking compared to the relatively short walk into Bramhall Lane earlier that day gave way to a shout from a fan towards the front of the small crowd of sodden supporters who recognised the same buildings we were passing for the second time.

An inquisitive and slightly agitated cry of "We're going round in circles here, the station's down there", aimed at both his fellow fans and our accompanying officers was greeted by silence as we continued past what looked like a sloped approach road to Sheffield station and the unmistakable lights and sounds of the busy terminus.

Sure enough, another 20 minutes later, we were brought to a stop at the top of the same road and told to file down it, close to the wall on the left hand side where we would have to wait until told to enter the station to board our train.

Finally, after standing in the increasingly heavy deluge, we were ushered silently along into the station entrance at the bottom of the access road, at which point the patience of one fan finally gave way.

"You did that on purpose didn't you?" he barked at the officer at the front of the escort as he passed him. Unmoved, apart from a noticeable grin appearing at the corners of his mouth, his resolve was finally snapped when another fan offered his two bob's worth:

"Were you bullied at school mate?" he sneered, leaning provocatively towards him.

As laughter rippled down the line, the Policeman span round, grabbing the fan by the shoulder of his coat, pulling him towards him.

"Yeah well you won't fuckin' come back 'ere in 'urry will ya" he spat in a Yorkshire drawl so broad it made Geoff Boycott and Fred Trueman sound like pre-war continuity announcers for the BBC.

As he released his grip on the fan, a disapproving roar rumbled through the ranks of fans.

Usually this type of incident would turn nasty very quickly, but he was quickly flanked by several of his fellow officers and with perfect timing another policeman appeared at the entrance to the station in front of us, shouting:

"MILLWALL TRAIN'S HERE…"

With that the crowd swarmed into the entrance to the station underpass towards the steps to the platform and our freezing cold football special, with a loud and defiant, but slightly damp "MMMMMMIIIIIIIIIILLLLLL…."

Over the coming years, if ever I felt the need to cheer my dad up for any reason, all I had to mention was that day in Sheffield. Just four simple words: "remember Sheffield United away?" was enough to ignite a gleam in his eyes and spread a knowing grin across his face. Back in 1987 it had merely been a way of ensuring I was able to make it to a Millwall away match, it ended up securing one of far too few but gratefully cherished memories between me and Dad.

7

THE NAUGHTY FORTY
AND GOING ON FIFTY

If Millwall were going to be playing in the First Division for the first time in 1988, the game's elite got a sneak preview of what to expect when QPR hosted them for a League Cup second round first leg. Despite falling 2-0 behind to their high-flying top flight opponents, the Lions fans, who seemed to outnumber the home support in the compact Loftus Road stadium by two to one, never relented in their unbelievable vocal support and were rewarded when Alan Walker crashed in a header with twelve minutes remaining setting it up nicely for the second leg at The Den, even though, as London derbies go, Millwall versus QPR didn't really set the fans' pulses racing.

Opinion on who were our true rivals was firmly split between West Ham and Crystal Palace. It was a question of where you lived and worked as many fans had dissipated from their Deptford, Bermondsey, Lewisham, Peckham or New Cross origins to various suburbs – either to the east or south. When we left our Balham flat just a few weeks after my first Millwall match, I was blissfully unaware that we were being relocated right in the middle of Crystal Palace territory.

By the time I was into my high school years I was fully aware of what it felt like to be either dreading or savouring a Monday morning following a defeat or win against your rivals.

According to my dad, the relationship between Millwall and Palace had been reasonably friendly, with West Ham being considered the sole enemy – until one November day in 1968. With both teams pushing for promotion to the First Division for the first time, Burt Head's Palace arrived at The Den in third place to face a Millwall side who had hit the top a few weeks earlier thanks to the talents of Derek Possee and Keith Weller. Unable to compete with The Lions on a skill level, Palace kicked their opponents off the park – which included an x-rated tackle on Millwall favourite Billy Neil – on their way to a 2-0 victory which signaled the demise of Millwall's promotion hopes and the birth of a simmering hatred for Crystal Palace among many Millwall fans.

Being one of only two Millwall fans at my school – the rest being mainly Palace, with a handful of Chelsea and Liverpool glory hunters who had never been near a football ground in their lives – victory in this game meant more to me than anything back in the 80s. It was the first fixture I looked out for when they were published in the summer and I looked forward to it with an equal mixture of dread and excitement. On the occasions we'd lost to them, I'd try anything to avoid facing the irritating sods back at school on Monday morning, even though I was never any good at pulling sickies or bunking off..

Naively, as we were splashing the cash in the summer, the match I was looking forward to the most in our unstoppable charge to the title was the inevitable thrashing of Palace. The reality was, of course, a tame 1-0 defeat where yet again our star striking duo failed to show up, while Wright and Bright dominated for Palace.

I spent the Saturday evening and all day Sunday feeling like a condemned man. Even if acting had been my forte, I'd need to be able to pull off an Oscar-winning performance to fool my mum enough to earn the whole week off and avoid the torment that the Palace fans at school had ready for me. It doesn't start straight away. You walk into the classroom and it's quiet. Maybe they've forgotten? Maybe they feel so thoroughly embarrassed by how they've robbed you of three points that they decide to stay quiet and call it quits. Of course not. The worst thing about it is the ones who start. It's the ones who have never been to a Palace game in their lives. Over-the-top cheering, clapping in your face, singing terrace chants that Palace fans don't even sing and getting the words wrong too. But that then gives the fans that were there, the ones that know they may have bragging rights but it was hardly the result of the year, to start.

Most of their enjoyment is gleaned from seeing how wound up I get from getting it in the ear from idiots who weren't even there. Then they engage in serious chat about the ins and outs of the match, how they were lucky to get the goal and how we'll probably be up there challenging at the end of the season, and you kid yourself the worst of it has passed. Only for them to revert to fully gloating mode again when the irksome gits who weren't there chirp up again. And so it goes on. You get it in the corridors as you make your way from one lesson to another and even the fans of other teams who are friends of the Palace mob get involved too.

I can remember the hatred building in my head: "Who do they think they are? Liverpool and Arsenal 'fans' who couldn't even name half the team that played their last game? Wankers." The resentment builds up and up inside you and you store it, hoping you'll have the opportunity to unleash it back to them later in the season after the return match. If I'm totally honest, I can take it from the fans who actually go and watch Palace, they have at least earned the right to give you stick, but the hangers-on, the hyenas, the fore-runner to the modern-day 'keyboard warrior' social media football troll or busy body who calls up 606 apoplectic with rage at why Arsene Wenger hasn't been sacked yet after introducing himself as a fan of 'Arsenal, Barcelona and Bayern Munich? They can do one.

To sum it up, probably the biggest Palace fan at my school, a lad called Terry, who was also in my year and went to every single Palace game home and away, would give me one little bit of stick when I first saw him after a Millwall defeat to Palace and then leave it at that.

Mercifully, I only had to endure the torment for one week – it would often last three or four. The following Monday morning saw me sat on a train heading out of south London into the posh leafy suburb of Purley at the start of two weeks of work experience at the Croydon Advertiser newspaper.

The long line of pupils filing into the office to discuss their work experience placements two weeks earlier fell into two distinct groups: the mickey-takers and couldn't-be-bothered brigade. The weary teacher in charge of sorting over two hundred children into two week stints at various local businesses was given various answers ranging from astronaut to catwalk model from the former category and was met with shrugs from the latter. Most of both found themselves seconded at various branches of local high street banks.

When I explained that I wanted to be a football journalist, she responded with a mixture of pleasant surprise that someone seemed to be taking the process half seriously and the sympathetic explanation that she wouldn't be able to achieve something quite that precise.

"You can't just be a football journalist" she explained, you need to work in general journalism and then work your way into sport".

Conscious that wasn't going to happen in two weeks, I gratefully accepted the offer of a stint at the local rag and looked forward to some time away from the usual school routine.

As soon as it became clear that I wasn't going to make it as a footballer I decided on what I considered to be the next best thing: writing about it. I liked the idea of being paid to go to football matches and file match reports or, better still, be one of those roaming correspondents that reported match updates back to the latest score radio shows like Sportswatch that had been the staple of so many Saturday afternoons for me and my dad over the years. The week I spent in the small newsroom at the Croydon Advertiser was pleasant enough. The Monday morning involved visiting the local police station with one of the reporters to be briefed on the events of the weekend to see if anything was newsworthy. Back then, Croydon was a quiet town full of estate agents and banks and there was nothing more juicy than a drunk and disorderly or burglary here and there to report. I imagine those meetings might produce a few more column inches thirty years on.

Slightly more interesting on that first drive down to Croydon nick was the reporter. A pretty blonde woman called Caroline, I guessed in her mid-twenties (although I was terrible and guessing age then and not much better now). She was exactly how you'd imagine a hungry young go-getting reporter to be: dynamic and confident with a tenacious desire to get the top scoop. I assumed that tagging a work experience kid along was the last thing she wanted to do but she seemed genuinely friendly towards me and obviously, being the 15-year-old testosterone whirlpool that I was, it didn't take long for me to start developing a bit of a crush on her.

In my mind, she was impressed by my boyish good looks coupled with my cool dress sense which belied my young school years. She probably thought I looked at least 18 – 20 at a push – and wouldn't hesitate to take me along to her favourite local wine bar to meet her high-flying friends at the end of a hard week's work. What a tale to tell the rest of the lads back at school in two weeks...

The truth of course was I was all Oxy 10 stains, Lynx Oriental and far too much hair gel, lost in an over-sized suit jacket and mismatched Chinos which had so obviously been paired with my regulation school shoes.

This reality was rammed home to me as I left the office at the end of the first day and, before the door could click shut behind me I heard Caroline's voice:
"Aww isn't he sweet? He only looks about twelve..." not quite the result I was looking for.

The rest of the week was spent turning a pile of rather uninspiring press releases into a few column inches of slightly more interesting reading. Some of it even made the week's editions, or found their way into one of the many free newspapers that the group produced and which I had spent many a long evening hour sticking through letterboxes in my neighbourhood for a few quid to fund my Millwall away trips.

When the final Friday arrived and the paper had been put to bed, the editor called me over to his desk and asked me to sit down. He asked if I'd enjoyed my time there, if I still wanted to be a journalist and if so, if there was any particular field I was interested in.

When I said "football", the editor spring to his feet and made for the door with an enthusiastic "follow me".

I tracked him through the maze of grey partitioned corridors and then up a narrow staircase into what seemed like a dark area in the roof space of the building. Holding open a door he ushered me in to a small room and then followed me in. It was a tiny makeshift office, thick with roll-up cigarette smoke – a smell I recognised from the Millwall terraces. It was dominated by a huge chest in the centre with narrow brass-handled drawers and on top of it the largest scrap book I had ever seen, laid open with dozens of newspaper cuttings pasted into it. On one side, facing the wall, were two desks with typewriters on, lit by green glass-shaded desk lamps, their orange light glowing through the Golden Virginia fog. The walls were plastered with more newspaper cuttings, scruffily scribbled notes and memos and calendars dating back to 1981. The point at which they met the desk was completely obscured with what looked like every edition of Rothman's Football Yearbook, intermingled with various cricketing volumes.

Two men, I guessed to be in their fifties, span round on squeaky swivel chairs from the desk as the door clicked shut behind us. Both looked like battle-hardened hacks that had seen it all. The editor introduced me, so quickly that I completely missed their names and with that, shook my hand and disappeared back out of the door. A little bemused, one of the men offered me a handshake, helpfully reintroduced himself as Derek and his colleague as Bob, then explained that this was where all of the newspaper's sports content was compiled. Noticing my fascination with the large chest and scrapbook, the other chap ambled over and showed me page after page of sporting headlines from years gone by, all pasted carefully into the pages for posterity and vital research purposes.

He showed me the coverage of Crystal Palace's 1976 FA Cup run where they reached the semi-finals as a Third Division club, the souvenir pull-out produced to celebrate their promotion to the First Division as Second Division champions in 1979 and reaching the top of the table under Terry Venables the following season when dubbed 'the team of the Eighties'.

Obviously assuming I was a Palace supporter but sensing my feigned enthusiasm, he sussed me out.

"I take it you're not a Palace fan then?" he breathed with a sense of anticipation at what my reply would be.

"No, I support Millwall" I offered, fully prepared for the usual response of us all being knuckle-dragging baby-eaters.

"Millwall? Bloody hell!" he laughed, "No wonder you weren't interested in all this lot! I don't blame you, I'm a Charlton fan, I bloody hate them. Bob here is more into his cricket".

I found the thought of Derek sat typing out epithets for Palace's latest win through gritted teeth quite amusing, although it was a dilemma that I had never considered. Not only could I not choose to be just a football journalist, I couldn't just report on Millwall matches and I was suddenly struck by the horrific image of being sent to report on Crystal Palace's triumphant FA Cup final win or – worse still, having to file copy about them beating my own beloved Lions.

As they made their way through several more roll-ups, we discussed our teams' various fortunes over the season so far. Charlton were newly promoted to the top flight that Millwall were so desperate to join and we quickly bonded on our mutual hatred for Crystal Palace, which had been intensified for Charlton fans since their ground share with them.

"It's a shame you didn't come and see us earlier in the week; you could've come with me to cover the Palace game on Wednesday."

Palace had played away to Aston Villa two days earlier and been hammered 4-1. I was absolutely gutted that I'd missed the chance to watch their humiliation free of charge from the comfort of the Villa Park press box.

It was typical of my luck. We said our goodbyes and I left them to their roll-ups and giant scrapbook. As I made my way out of the door, Derek offered his hand once again. As I had the door handle in my right hand, I instinctively offered my left hand to his, the hand that I'd been hiding. The hand with the freshly scabbed cuts on the knuckles. Derek noticed it straight away and with a smile said:

"Hope the other bloke came off worse than you".

He must have assumed the cuts had been the result of a fight, and, being a Millwall fan, draw the obvious but very wrong conclusion. The reality was far less dramatic.

The night of that Palace hammering was instead spent at home, Millwall were playing Plymouth away and the routine for following The Lions on a midweek game if you couldn't be there was slightly different to the weekend ritual. There were no live updates to follow on the radio, if you were lucky the half time score might get a mention on the news. Thanks to teletext though, you could follow the goals within minutes of them going in of course and, if you were one of just a few games being played, you were afforded the luxury of having your latest scores on a single page, meaning you didn't lose your team's score while the other pages of matches scrolled through. There was one other wonderful little advantage to this too: The update feature.

The way teletext worked was that once you clicked back to the TV, it would go back to the index page – usually 100. You could program it to be set to a specific page number as the index – for our purposes in 1987 it was page

140 for the football index – a bit like setting your favourite home page on your Internet browser nowadays.

However, a new feature back in 1987 (on our television set at least) was the update button which, if pressed while you were on a certain page, saved that page when you clicked back on to teletext. Better than that, if the page changed, you got a little alert – the page number would appear in a little black box at the top right of your TV screen.

Now obviously this was no good if you pressed it on a Saturday when there were four or more pages of scrolling latest scores as it would keep popping up every time it went to a new page. But, if there was just one page of latest scores – as there was on this occasion – this genius little invention was there to let you know someone had scored – because obviously the page has 'changed' when they update the scores.

You might be wondering why we wouldn't just leave the page on as we did on Saturdays. That's because the TV would have an alternative use on Tuesdays or Wednesdays. These were the only nights league football was played in the English league back in the 80s, with the exception of Stockport or Tranmere who played home games on a Friday night occasionally to avoid clashes with Liverpool, Everton, Manchester United and Manchester City and boost their gates. Football on Monday or Thursday was considered far too ridiculous to conceive.

Tuesday or Wednesday TV schedules weren't crammed with soaps as they are today, midweek staples such as This is Your Life, Last of the Summer Wine or Boon were the order of the day in 1987 and were just some of the programmes of choice for my mum. So a combination of Millwall away in a midweek fixture and Mum settling down for an evening's TV became a living room battle zone.

Hostilities would commence around 7:25pm when she'd be settling into her favourite arm chair with a cup of tea, ready to see who Eamon Andrews would be thrusting his red book at next while I'd be reaching for the remote to call up the latest score page and quickly pressing the 'update' button, resuming normal service before she could complain. All was well until that moment when you notice the screen flicker out of the corner of your eye and the '141' appear in its little box in the top right of the screen.

"Dad, goal" I'd announce, reaching for the remote.

Dad would look up from his newspaper or book (he was never a television fan and only in the room to worship the update button otherwise he'd be in the kitchen with his radio).

In an instant, Mum's viewing of a funny anecdote about the time the subject of this week's show's wig fell off when he was meeting the Queen would be brought to a halt and replaced with a black screen announcing the score.

That exact scenario played out that night, and as I tapped the 'Text' button, Nirvana was revealed: Plymouth 0, Millwall 1 (Cascarino, 24)

It was followed by shouts of celebration meaning even the audio was rendered redundant for poor old Mum. Once we had regained our composure, reminding ourselves there was "a long time to go yet..." we sat back down, only to be reminded by Mum that the teletext page was still on screen, which was remedied by Mum angrily pressing the 'TV' button on the remote, thus cancelling the all-important 'update' feature. We then sat there blissfully unaware that communications with Plymouth were now down and, if there were any further goals, we'd be none the wiser, until of course we realised and back on went the Teletext, clicking through to the latest scores page, ready to set it to update again.

Mum's complaints were drowned out this time by the realisation that there had indeed been another goal – an equaliser for the home team – resulting in cursing and swearing about Millwall's inability to hold a lead and how the inevitable defeat was now coming. Once again, both sound and vision were rendered useless for Mum's evening TV entertainment.

Sometimes the update function would mess you about. It would appear, but when you clicked on to the page nothing had changed. Sometimes, you wondered if it had reset itself.

"Is it broke? Check to see if it's still on the right page…"

All of this added to Mum's evening of frustration and accelerated the previously unheard of concept in our house: a second television.

Just as things seem to settle down and it appeared Millwall were heading for a useful away point and Mum could finally enjoy the strains of Jim Diamond's 'Hi Ho Silver', the screen flickered again and the number appeared.

I nudged my dad and pointed at the screen, then looked at the clock.

"There's only about 15 minutes left – do you reckon it's us?" I teased, desperate to find out if we had scored a winner, terrified to learn we'd conceded again but also wary that the score would still say 1-1.

Reaching for the remote, I slowly pressed the 'Text' button and waited.

"Plymouth 1, Millwall 2 (Cascarino 24, Sheringham 76)

Instinctively I leapt up to celebrate, almost as if I'd seen the goal go in from the away terrace, I thrust my left fist up above me and instantly felt a sharp pain.

The pain in my hand was followed immediately by a rather unnerving "POP" which echoed around the now darkened room and was followed by a very faint burning smell. As my mum shrieked with greatly-exaggerated terror and my dad started to curse and swear, rolling his eyes as he surveyed the damage to the light fitting, I tried to juggle my emotions between the pain of my injury, the joy of Millwall scoring what looked like a late winner and attempting to appease my angry dad. My celebratory fist-pump had pushed the brass hanging light fitting into the ceiling and obviously smashed the bulb. Dad shone a torch on the scene and cursed some more as he surveyed the buckled light and black scorched ceiling, while Mum continued complaining about the disruption to her evening's television viewing.

Attempts to calm my dad were fruitless, even noticing the teletext page had now changed again to confirm our victory with a satisfying "FT" to the right of the score. Dad, being Dad, was still there an hour later with his wooden stepladder and dust sheet, carefully applying emulsion to cover the ceiling burns after managing to bend the light fitting back into some sort of normal shape even though, in his words, "it looked like Uri bleedin' Geller had been at it…".

I could still hear him messing about downstairs way past eleven as I lay in bed, trying to ignore the throbbing pain in my knuckles, but consoling myself with a very good away win – and long overdue goals from Cascarino and Sheringham. Maybe, just maybe, the season was starting to take off? I'd often heard relatives use the expression "after the Lord Mayor's show…" and never understood what it meant. Only when I started to follow Millwall was the true meaning revealed to me – on countless occasions.

To bring you statistically up to speed, our win at Plymouth had seen us nestle nicely in fifth place – a morale-boosting leap of five places since that horrible defeat at Palace. Two relatively straightforward wins lay ahead of us we assumed, before our first big test of the season away to Aston Villa. Huddersfield were bottom of the table, still without a league win to their name and would seven days after hosting Millwall, travel to Manchester City and lose 10-1. Yet somehow, in a Halloween horror show so typical of Millwall, we managed to hand them a 2-1 win.

The beauty of English football is of course the way the fixtures come thick and fast and just three days later we had the chance to put things right with a home match against a very ordinary Bournemouth side who would no doubt feel the wrath of that stinging loss in Yorkshire and help limber us up for our daunting trip to the Midlands.

I bought my tickets for the trip to Villa before the game and took my place on the halfway line terrace alongside Dad and the usual crew. The regulars were obviously me and my dad, along with Steve and his dad Terry. I had managed to persuade my dad that the halfway line offered a better vantage point for the match and he reluctantly sacrificed his favourite spot behind the Cold Blow Lane goal so that we could join a larger group of fellow fans and friends. Stuart and his dad Ernie were family friends of Steve and Terry. Stuart was the same age as Steve and, just half a dozen or so games into the season, felt like we'd known each other for years. The football terraces had that effect on friendships, accelerating their development through the mutual love of the team, cemented by a common enjoyment of moaning about the state of affairs on the pitch and providing a permanent bond and appreciation that belied spending just a couple of hours together every two weeks. As the season went on our number would grow.

The first half against Bournemouth was one of those matches where you wondered if the players actually knew this was a league match, being played for points and counting towards their salaries. The team had to be reshuffled as Terry Hurlock was missing through injury and replaced by Keith Stevens. Stevens, nicknamed 'Rhino' for his no-nonsense bustling style was another home grown prospect who had made the right back position his own but had been displaced by Danis Salman earlier in the season. Stevens looked a little nervous in his unfamiliar midfield role alongside Les Briley, but he wasn't the only one. Motions were gone through, lost causes were given up on, tackles made half-heartedly and as the players trouped off for their break, the Millwall fans made it very clear what they thought of the first half's endeavours.

Millwall folklore tells us that Teddy Sheringham, the apparent darling of The Den, one-time record goal scorer, moulded from the club's own youth policy who would go on to great things for club and country both home and abroad, was offered sage advice as he left the pitch that evening. In his autobiography, Tony Cascarino tells how he was bought by Millwall as the experienced centre forward. The old head to cosset young gun Teddy.

However he quickly learned that this was not the case – made apparent on their very first league game together at Middlesbrough when he said Sheringham was bossing him about constantly. Cascarino was admittedly wary of the Millwall crowd. He would be the first to admit that his move hadn't gone well. Goals had not come as freely as they were expected and Sheringham's form also seemed to have dipped from the previous season, prompting worries - even from the families of the players themselves apparently – that the two were not compatible on the football pitch.

This was something which, if true, would certainly be fatal to any promotion aspirations. Cascarino was understandably apprehensive whenever he came in close proximity to the Millwall fans who, as I'm sure you and the entire footballing world knows, are not shy at expressing an opinion.

As a striker your natural central position on the pitch meant that you could avoid the fans' angst at close quarters. You didn't have to take corners and rarely took throw-ins so you were spared a one-on-one discussion with a supporter who felt that you should have perhaps done a little better with that chance earlier. Walking off at half time or at the end of a match at The Den was a very different matter though.

Unlike most grounds, the players' tunnel at the original Den was behind the goal at the Cold Blow Lane End. Players and officials were therefore left to run the gauntlet from the Millwall terraces which were perched unnervingly close to pitch-side. There was no sanctuary of a player exit disappearing into a fancy main stand with the vacated seats of corporate hangers on who had long since decanted into the bar surrounding it.

As the players trudged back to the dressing room surrounded by a chorus of boos and chants of "Shit, shit, shit…" Cascarino and Sheringham cut very different figures on their way to the tunnel. Cascarino kept his head down, to avoid eye contact and, I'm sure, did his best to blot out the insults. The more cavalier Sheringham on the other hand was having none of it and, shoulders back, head high, faced the throng with typical bullishness, but as he strode into the dark safety of the tunnel he was left with the following words of advice ringing in his ears:

"Oi Sheringham, get that fucking piano off your back…"

It didn't work. The second half actually achieved the unthinkable in being worse than the first. A very poor Bournemouth side took the lead early on and Millwall were playing the sort of football that prompted the well-worn cliché from my dad that they wouldn't score if they were playing until midnight. This observation might have carried more weight if he didn't trot it out five goalless minutes after watching Millwall fall behind.

Not for the first time, Dad was wrong. They did score. With the game moving into the last ten minutes and Bournemouth looking like they couldn't believe their luck at how easily they were escaping The Den with a win, a goalmouth scramble ended with Cascarino toe-poking the ball over the line. As he followed the ball into the net to retrieve it – that favourite gesture of players who have scored a desperately-needed goal to hopefully mark a grand comeback as if to say "right let's make sure we put the ball back on the centre spot quicker so that we can get another one…" he looked up at the cheering Millwall fans behind the Cold Blow Lane goal that he had scored in and shook a snarling clenched fist at them.

This was almost unheard of at Millwall, and would normally elicit a very bad response. Given Cascarino's evident lack of self-confidence however, it was seen as a brave act of passionate defiance and they cut him a well-deserved break, this could be the turning point in his Millwall career – the entire season, this could be the comeback that finally got the promotion train back on the rails.

With almost the last kick of the game, Millwall left back Nicky Coleman slipped, allowing Bournemouth striker Dave Shearer in to score the winner. Boos once again filled the air as the players left the pitch at full time just seconds later, this time Coleman was getting the full brunt of it.

I felt sorry for Coleman. Another product of the youth team, he was a local lad, a Millwall supporter and solid defender. He quickly became the easy scapegoat for most of the team's defensive failings, but what most of the Den regulars didn't see were his performances away from home which were completely different. As a youngster playing for the club he loved, you can totally understand the pressure he felt playing in front of the terraces where he had himself once stood.

This defeat was typical Millwall. That's what we told ourselves. In truth it was typical football. You nick a great win away from home, and then lose the next two.

I'm ashamed to admit that, on the way out of the ground, I jogged up to the ticket office window, rapped on it and, when a flustered woman appeared in front of me, I asked if I could get a refund for my ticket to Aston Villa.

"No refunds" was the abrupt reply, and the window slammed shut in my face. It was a single moment of disloyal weakness which I regret even now looking back at it.

I was travelling to Villa "with a mate". Dad put up no argument. As much as he had enjoyed Sheffield United away, he didn't fancy being corralled into another away day and suspected I'm sure that I was travelling solo.

The usual feeling of excitement and anticipation was missing as the football special pulled into Witton and we were led by Police escort on the short walk to Villa Park. After the Bournemouth debacle, this would surely be one of the final nails in our promotion coffin.

Villa Park was an impressive stadium, worthy of Division One football, but looking and sounding very second rate with just 13,000 in it. You sensed that maybe there was a chance for us to do something here. The feeling of doom and gloom that seemed to envelop both supporters and team from the first whistle at the home game with Bournemouth was thrown off. Maybe it was the pressure of The Den?

Within 20 minutes we were 2-0 up, sparking the sort of goal celebrations that are a delicious mixture of elation and total joyous surprise. The inevitable Villa goal came soon after but Millwall held on to claim a famous victory. Cascarino had scored the first and looked a different player, as did Coleman. Stevens showed his versatility by completely bossing the midfield alongside Briley and made just his second game of the season in an unfamiliar position look like he'd been doing it for years. To be honest, the role was made for him, as he excelled in being the spoiler that the position demanded. You could tell he loved to break up play and knock a nice little ball forward to the waiting Cascarino, or ping one out to a waiting winger. More importantly, he also knew when to just play it simple, a little sideways pass to Briley to take the heat out of the situation when needed.

We left with choruses of "If you're all going to West Ham clap your hands" anticipating the midweek Simod Cup tie three days later, suddenly full of confidence that this team really could cut it. The Simod Cup was a competition designed to provide competition for teams in the top two divisions following the ban on English teams playing in Europe which UEFA enforced after the Heysel Stadium riot in 1985. Understandably, no-one cared and attendances were woeful. This was an era in football where clubs were struggling to attract decent attendances to league games let alone tin-pot trophies played on bleak Tuesday nights in November.

There was the incentive of a Wembley final, something none of us had seen with Millwall, but as West Ham took the lead early in the second half the twin towers seemed farther away than ever for The Lions. It was a shame because, if the competition hadn't quite captured the imagination of the West Ham fans, Millwall's supporters were certainly determined to make the most of the first meeting between the two bitter rivals in almost ten years. Just over 11,000 were spread out around Upton Park, apart from the away section behind the goal. The Chicken Run as it was known was packed and when Cascarino struck the equaliser with fifteen minutes left it erupted.

I remember being so packed into that terrace that jumping up and down was almost impossible, but once you got your arms above your head, you just let yourself ride along the wave of madness. The euphoria was such that we were still in the final throes of celebrating the first goal when the second one came, this time from Sheringham. We were in dreamland. The West Ham fans in the adjacent stand tried to give the impression that they weren't bothered about such a pointless competition, something that the rows and rows of empty seats around us as our cheers and songs echoed around the sparsely populated stadium seemed to underline. But they knew, as we did, that this had nothing to do with the competition. It didn't matter if it was the Simod Cup, FA Cup or flicking tiddlywinks into a plastic cup, this was Millwall v West Ham. It meant so much more than any mere categorisation of event. They knew it, it hurt, and it was beautiful.

Four days later Leeds were despatched 3-1 at The Den, courtesy of a second half Cascarino hat-trick. His performances at Villa and West Ham had pumped him full of self-belief and that, displayed in front of the Millwall fans at a vociferous Den against such eagerly awaited opponents as Leeds, was as powerful as the criticism can be debilitating if they sense inferiority as they had done from Cascarino in his earlier games. There are no half measures with Millwall fans, if you're not playing well, you're shit. If you're playing well, you're worshipped, and it must make you feel invincible.

Stoke away came next. When the travel and match tickets had gone on sale I had big plans to treat my dad for his birthday which was a few weeks before the match. It would be Dad's 49th birthday, a scary number for me. In my mind, my dad was entering his last year of 'not being old'. Fifty was *old* old. Then there was the spectre of his dad's death at 51 that haunted me too. Dad's usual dismissal of "They never win there", when I said I was going was this time accompanied by a sterner warning of trouble from Stoke's hooligan element which meant that persuading him to go would be impossible so I didn't bother, Steve was more than happy to have his tickets.

Following Millwall away had become routine now. Everything I needed, my football travelling survival kit, sat on my bedside table. The latest match programme with details of the next away match, playing cards for the journey, cash to spend and, of course, the all-important train tickets for the 'football special'.

Talk of trouble from rival fans didn't bother me, you always felt safe travelling with Millwall. There was much talk of Stoke's 'Naughty Forty' hooligans making an appearance on the journey up there but no hint of them was seen or heard all day.

I travelled with Steve for this one on the football special train again. The only nerves I felt was during the underground connection on the way to Euston that morning. Three days earlier 31 people had died as fire ripped through Kings Cross tube station. As long as I could remember I'd used the London Underground and totally taken for granted its quick and easy way of moving speedily hundreds of feet below London's streets. I never considered how it could become such a horrifying death trap during an emergency.

Once above ground, emerging onto the Euston Station concourse was quite a sight on a Saturday morning during the football season in the late 1980s. The football supporter's main outfit of choice was clear for all to see. Everywhere you looked there were young men in black leather jackets, faded jeans and white Hi-Tec Squash trainers. A copy of the day's tabloid paper of choice would often be added, folded and placed inside the back pocket, ready for the journey ahead. This wasn't just Millwall supporters. Fans of a variety of London clubs would all be wandering around, checking which platform they were due to leave from, grabbing food and drink for the two or three hour ride north. It used to amaze me how there was never any trouble. Stations are of course a hotbed for football fights, because of the very nature of how they – especially Euston – bring different teams' fans all together at the same time. The early Saturday morning it seemed subdued would-be hooligans however. They were too delicate perhaps, nursing a hangover from the previous night's adventures and, with them yet to have the fire in their bellies that the day's football action would provide, rather more keen on a bacon roll than a punch-up.

Stoke's Victoria Ground stadium was what I considered a 'proper football ground', in the same way Millwall's Den was. It rose up amongst the terraced houses of the community it served and you could sense the history of the place. So much had been untouched and lift just-so throughout the good times gone by, almost out of a sense of loyalty, like when parents refuse to touch anything in the bedroom of a missing child. I guess the truth behind that rather extreme comparison is that, back in the 70s and 80s, football clubs felt no need to spend money that they either didn't have or could spend elsewhere on tarting up their stands. Not only that but many were still great tributes to architectural greats such as Archibald Leitch. The name probably means nothing to you – it certainly meant nothing to me back in 1987, but he is the man responsible for many of the classic old stadium features that we became so familiar with in our days watching Match of the Day in the 70s and 80s – 'The Shelf' at Tottenham's White Hart Lane is a great example - and are so sadly lacking in today's plastic and breeze block new-builds.

I've always been puzzled why football teams do so much better at home than away. I know it should be obvious that a home team has many advantages – not least playing in familiar surroundings with the better support behind them, but is that really enough to give them an actual advantage great enough to enable them to win the game – even if the opposition are superior? It seems so. Millwall have a history of struggling away from home but being hard to beat at The Den and you have to put that down to the uniqueness of the ground and its variety of unwelcoming aspects for visiting players and fans. In his famous book 'Only A Game' Millwall player Eamon Dunphy spoke about his experience of both sides of the fence. He had visited The Den as a York City player and told of how the away changing rooms were smaller, more dingy, then of the intimidation of the home fans which just made you want to get back on the coach and go home. Then he signed for Millwall and the experience of playing at The Den was completely different. At Stoke, the home fans weren't exactly roaring their team on, but Millwall's players looked a very long way from home for the first 45 minutes. At half time we trailed 1-0 and it felt as though our recent purple patch may be coming to an end. It was hard to see where a sustained run of good results was going to come from to keep us up with the chasing pack.

Millwall emerged from the break a changed team and within ten minutes of the restart Cascarino had equalised. Stoke's defenders looked panic-stricken every time he got near the ball, using his body to expertly shield it while other players came into play, feinting one way, turning the other, all he needed was another goal. We were stood at the back of the shallow paddock away terrace of Stoke's old Victoria ground. It was a fairly small but lively away following and as we entered the final ten minutes you could sense something was about to happen.

Again Cascarino found himself with his back to goal just inside the Stoke penalty area and as he twisted and turned in an attempt to unshackle himself from his Stoke markers, he managed to wriggle free for a split second and whittle enough room to swing a yellow-socked foot at the ball. Completely wrong-footed, the Stoke 'keeper could only watch as the ball bounced once in front of him and then past him into the net.

I remember jumping up and then watching the perimeter fence hurtle towards my face with my feet completely off the ground, only coming to rest at the foot of the terrace, cushioned by a variety of elbows, shoulders and backs. I lost Steve for a few seconds, only to see his face suddenly appear in front of me, then disappear again. I can only describe it as being how I'd imagine it to be if you were involved in a high speed train crash, but obviously much more fun. I appreciate that somewhat inappropriate comparison only goes to underline the danger of football terraces – borne out a couple of years later at Hillsborough – but at that time, the terror that I should have felt by being completely out of control of my body in a mass of other limbs and the imminent threat of being crushed or pummeled into a wall or fence was completely usurped by the sheer joy of seeing my team score a late goal away from home.

The Police escort back to Stoke station was understandably upbeat, and the officers charged with the thankless task of shepherding a couple of hundred smug Londoners out of their town were surprisingly better-humoured than their south Yorkshire colleagues a couple of months before. Even when the convoy was accompanied by a chorus of "Maybe it's because I'm a Londoner" which was quickly rehashed to "Maybe it's because I'm a northerner, that I wear Lionel Blairs…" and punctuated by shouts of "outside toilet" and "what a shithole" aimed at residents who dared to peek out of the windows of their terraced houses as we passed.

Now up to seventh, we really had to make this away win count when third paced Hull visited The Den a week later. An easy 2-0 win came courtesy of Sheringham and not Cascarino this time, but the goal drought was only temporary with "Cas" as he was now affectionately referred to on target again with two more in an easy midweek win over Reading, sending Millwall into the top three for the first time that season.

Millwall were running riot – in the best possible way. It was surely only a matter of time before top spot was ours, starting with mid-table Blackburn away. What could go wrong?

8
THE FAIRY TALE OF NEW CROSS

My earliest and most lucid childhood memories are of my dad. Even though my mum was the constant figure in my life and was at home every day looking after me while Dad went out to work, if I cast my mind back as far as I can, my most vivid recollection is my fascination watching my dad. He was meticulous in everything he did. Whether it was washing, shaving or even making a cup of tea, there was an almost hypnotic precision about the way he went about it. I could feel the concentration he was putting into each stroke of the razor or the way he set the laces on his shoes neatly to one side when taking them off after work.

It was as if he was trying to perform each task in the face of irritating distraction, like trying to recall a telephone number while hundreds of people shouted random digits in your ears. Like most boys, I watched and I copied. At school getting changed for P.E. I would carefully lay the laces on my school shoes uniformly to one side.

"Why do you do that?" my teacher Mrs Baten once enquired.

"Because my dad does" I replied. Mrs Baten smiled and nodded understandingly.

Sometimes, watching Dad would even distract me from my own world. I would often turn away from my pile of toys on the living room floor or Top of The Pops on the television to see Dad in his most familiar pose: slumped in the chair, hand across his brow, looking blankly into the distance. Dad had perfected his own version of the thousand yard stare, interrupted only by solemn slow shakes of the head. Curious, I would always ask him what was wrong. His reaction to this was varied. Often he would shake himself out of his daze, smile weakly and reply "nothing" in an unusually soft tone.

Dad, like all dads, had a booming voice, one that could be heard through the house, whether it was shouting in anger, laughing with joy or merely talking in regular conversation. All Dads boom, it's what they're supposed to do. I took everything my dad did as 'what Dads where supposed to do'. They got up early in the morning, whistled loudly while they washed and shaved, left the house before anyone else was up and returned home in the evening just as dinner was being served. They read the newspaper in the chair and tutted at the Nine O'Clock News. One day, asking my dad what was wrong got me into trouble at school – and I didn't even understand why.

I was six years old and the school day always ended the same way: story time. It was by far the best part of the day for me, not just because it was almost home time, but because I loved stories. More than that, I loved to escape and stories helped me do just that. I loved to close my eyes and transport myself to the land and characters they described. I was fixed to Jackanory on the television after arriving home and story time at the end of the school day was a perfect taster for this.

One particularly warm afternoon I was sat on the carpeted area at the front of the class with the rest of my schoolmates listening to our teacher Mrs Baten reading the latest tale. I could feel my eyes closing, partly through the enjoyment of the story and partly through the fatigue of another long school day. I was suddenly aware that Mrs Baten had stopped reading and the class was silent, only punctuated by a stifled giggle or two.

"Oh Mervyn" Mrs Baten chided playfully, "You poor thing, you look like you're ready for your bed".

Almost without thinking I replied:

"I feel like doing myself in"

Mrs Baten's mood immediately changed.

"That's a terrible thing to say, don't ever let me hear you say anything like that again".

I was shocked at this response. What was so wrong with that?

During the weekend before, my dad was once again slumped in the chair. As usual, I asked him what was wrong, to which he replied "Nothing" as usual.

Moments later I heard him speak again, I wasn't sure if he was talking to me, but there was no-one else in the room. He mumbled under his breath but I could clearly make out the words:

"I feel like doing myself in".

I asked him what it meant but he didn't reply.

A bit unnerved, I went to ask my mum, who rather awkwardly replied that it was simply another way of saying you were very tired. She was of course trying to protect me. What mother would explain to her child that his father could really have meant by that? So, like most little boys growing up who want to be like their dads, I did my very own impression of him a few days later in school as soon as the opportunity arose – and was completely dumbfounded by the result.

Nothing was said about the episode again, and I managed to blank it out of my mind for the rest of my childhood, although it would come back to haunt me in my adult years.

It would be almost four decades before we would finally join up the dots between Dad's obsessive tidiness, his long periods of silence, early nights, irritability and general dark moods. In between there would of course be some chinks of light, love and laughter. Dad was dealing with his demons in the best way he knew how. On the outside, it looked like he was struggling. The reality was, when we learned the true depth of his suffering, we realised he had dealt with it with unbelievable strength.

We became used to Dad's 'quiet moments'. We acknowledged that there were times when he would just slump in the chair and say nothing for hours on end. We put it down to tiredness – just as Mum had explained to me all those years before. As an impatient teenager for whom life was very cut and dried, I accepted that Dad was a grumpy bugger when he went to work Monday to Friday and moaned about the trains and Margaret Thatcher, did his little jobs around the house or in the garden at the weekends and spent hours dozing or staring into the distance in his chair in between. I started to ignore those bits of Dad, and just engaged with him when it was time to go to a Millwall match – or follow them on the radio. He was different then, it was like putting new batteries in an electronic toy.

Dad was in position in his chair after a Saturday morning of pottering about the house and wasn't responding much to my conversation-starters about our prospects away to in-form Blackburn that day. I recognised the signs and felt it best to keep out of the way. For all the 'tired' excuses we satisfied ourselves with in explaining his behaviour, there was something worrying about it, but we buried our heads in the sand. I knew he'd probably liven up by kick-off time, but fancied a change of scenery.

October and November had cleaned me out financially. There's only so far three paper rounds and a fiver-a-week pocket money will stretch. Tickets, travel, food and drink to the west Midlands, east London and Stoke - that peculiar part of the country that no-one outside of it knows quite where it is, meant that Blackburn away was a non-starter. The home brewing kit I'd bought for my dad's birthday back in October had seen off the last of the cash stash, but I was hoping that, come Christmas, it'd be paying for itself in delicious, free, home-made amber nectar.

So, instead of sampling the delights of Lancashire, re-enacting a Lowry painting and 'going to the match', I shunned the mental torture of sitting in front of teletext with Dad's radio for the more bizarre option of Croydon town centre.

Getting a draw at Blackburn wouldn't have been the end of the world. Losing at Blackburn wouldn't have been the end of the world. Losing at Blackburn and then having your record-signing striker who had suddenly hit red hot form and was banging in goals for fun taken off injured was the sort of gargantuan kick in the knackers that only following Millwall could inflict upon you it seemed.

I met up with Steve and we got the train to West Croydon at lunchtime. We took the short walk past the Odeon cinema and its queues for the first showing of Superman 4, Dirty Dancing and Beverley Hills Cop II and made for the recently-opened Pizza Hut restaurant. Whilst Saturday afternoon in Croydon may sound like some sort of low grade punishment dished out to petty criminals made to wear high viz vests and pick up litter or clean graffiti off walls, it was a regular past-time that both Steve and I enjoyed because it afforded a few rare perks to young teenage life.

For a start, Pizza Hut sold beer. Or to be more precise, beautiful large ice cold tankards of cool crisp Heineken, and the waiting staff, who barely spoke or understood a word of English that wasn't on the menu, happily served us with two pints of the stuff each to accompany our food.

Then there was 'birds'. Steve always felt a Saturday afternoon trip to Croydon was great for 'picking up birds', but this never happened, and 'eyeing them up' as he liked to call it only made you look like some sort of sex pest. God knows what would happen to us these days.

Whilst window shopping was something that you'd expect women to favour as a weekend pastime, we still enjoyed perusing the many clothes, records and electronics shops, looking for rare import music, the latest top clobber and lavish stereos – none of which were within our flimsy budgets.

On this particular Saturday there was of course a football match going on. After burping away through the last of our pepperoni special, we walked to the Whitgift Centre shopping precinct. We then spent the next two hours mooching around the shops, with absolutely no intention of buying anything, then heading into the Sound and Vision department of Alders to get a score update from Ewood Park on teletext.

Yep, instead of sitting in the comfort of my own living room, I chose to spend what few quid I had left on a train ticket to Croydon and stroll aimlessly around a cold shopping centre full of weary husbands being dragged around for the early Christmas shop, pissed up winos and screaming kids, only to check my team's latest score on a TV in a packed department store.

We made it to Alders for the first check at about ten past three to discover Millwall were already one nil down. Our disdain was interrupted by an eager television salesman who was keen to go through every set available to a mockingly inquisitive Steve, who could never resist a wind-up. After eagerly explaining they had "a 26 incher arriving next week", Steve thanked him but said he was perfectly happy with his twelve incher – as was his girlfriend – and we made our way down to Surrey Street Market to kill some time going through the Aladdin's cave of records at Beano's second had record store. Guessing we wouldn't be made very welcome back in Alders, we made our way to Rumbelows for the second half score check.

"YES! 1-1 Cascarino, get in!" came Steve's shout as the latest score page flicked into life. The Millwall goal machine had done it again, and with 25 minutes left, there was surely time for a winner – just as he had done at Stoke. I felt elated and distraught in one go. I wished I had gone.

"Let's just stay here till the end" Steve decided. I agreed, the sadness of the whole situation, like a crap episode from a juvenile delinquent version of Last of the Summer Wine, was temporarily lost on me in the excitement of waiting for another famous win to be carved out in neon on the screen in front of us.

We stood there, hypnotised by the pages of latest scores flicking from one to the next, until, just as we waited for 4/4 to change back and reveal the latest update from Blackburn, the screen went black.

We span round to see a smug-looking middle-aged chap holding the TV remote as if it was the holy grail.

"Are we interested in buying today sirs?" he enquired in a whiny nasal tone that sounded like a buzz saw.

"Er, yeah" started Steve, "We were just checking the teletext works, you know. Can you whack it back on for us please?"

Silently, with a slow shake of the head, he popped the remote in his trouser pocket, patted it and walked slowly away. This was the problem with following the latest Millwall scores in Croydon.

"Fuckin' Palace wanker" Steve coughed as we nudged past the jobsworth assistant on our way out and made our way quickly across the road and back to Alders.

By the time we made it there and found a TV, managed to find the correct remote and prodded the numbers in for the latest scores, it was all over. Blackburn had scored a second just as our friendly salesman in Rumbelows was pulling the plug and it had finished 2-1 to the home team.

The tin hat on an all-round disaster of a day was well and truly shoved on top when, on arriving home I discovered from Dad that, soon after equalising, Cascarino had gone off with what looked like a nasty injury. It would be three days before we found out via the Tuesday edition of the South London Press that he had sustained a rib injury that would keep him out for about four weeks. It was a complete disaster and surely the end of our automatic promotion hopes at least.

Leeds were beaten again a few days later in the Simod Cup. What a competition eh? It had managed to draw West Ham v Millwall and then

Millwall v Leeds in its first two rounds. A Policeman's overtime wet dream. Almost as if to raise hope that we could manage without Cascarino, goals from Sheringham and Walker gave us a 2-0 win to progress to the next round and set us up for the league visit of Manchester City to The Den and revenge we hoped for that 4-0 thumping earlier in the season.

After a slow start, City were starting to live up to the early season billing as promotion favourites and were two places behind Millwall in eighth place. They arrived with a noisy, large away following, boosting The Den crowd to one of the largest league gates in a few years. The Man City players were hard to miss too, in a bizarre red and black checked kit. Unfortunately, the Millwall defence managed to miss one of them: their new singing Tony Adcock, who complemented his tablecloth style shirt with a shock of bright ginger hair, drawing the obvious cat calls of derision from the Millwall crowd. Adcock laughed last though, scoring the only goal of the game on the stroke of half time.

Seven days later we travelled to Barnsley and were thumped 4-1. Our top scorer was gone, and it looked like the defence had decided to finish early for Christmas too. A sad footnote to the match was that it would prove to be an end to the Millwall career of Paul Sansome. The Goalkeeper who had taken over from Peter Wells under George Graham and made himself a firm favourite with fans was in for the injured Brian Horne and, with Horne only needing a one game break, the heavy defeat was to prove the final Millwall league game for a loyal goalkeeper who I can never really remember having a bad game for the club. He left for Southend shortly after that game.

It was a defeat that sent us spinning down to ninth place, and seemed to undo all that good work in November.

Without realising, football, more precisely Millwall, was starting to take over my life. My mood from Saturday afternoon to Wednesday or Thursday was being dictated by their weekend result. The 4-1 defeat at Barnsley I decided, had ruined Christmas. As I drifted slowly down the escalator at Alders after buying presents for my mum and dad on Christmas Eve, the strains of The Pogues' new single, 'Fairytale of New York' rang out around me and Shane McGowan's bleak opening lines struck a chord. Things had really turned ugly.

We took our first tentative sips of our newly opened home-brew lager just as the Boxing Day matches were kicking off. Far from being amber nectar, it was a peculiar dark colour. What little head it had after pouring quickly popped and died like the last lingering bubbles in a luke-warm bath tub. The only encouraging part was that the clay-like sludgy bits (which I confidently told Dad was 'the sediment', even though I had absolutely no idea what 'sediment' was) didn't make it from the bottom of the giant white container which we had stored in the cupboard under the stairs through the tap and into the glass.

We kidded ourselves that the first few sips were surprisingly tasty and forced more insipid mouthfuls down as we keenly watched the latest scores pop up on screen. By the 75th minute we had to wonder if this potent moonshine was having hallucinatory effects, which was unlikely, given that we'd only managed to down about an eighth of a pint each. Either way, we felt like we were experiencing some sort of weird fantasy-like vision. The score from The Hawthorns read: West Bromwich Albion 1, Millwall 4.

Forty Eight hours later we were back at The Den to see another Cascarino-less goal fest as Millwall raced into a 3-0 half time lead against Sheffield United. Even Robbie Cooke, the short-term replacement for Cascarino brought in from Brentford and, in all fans' eyes, totally inadequate and derided in every game he started, managed to get in on the act.

We'd finished the year on a high, but it was a knackering, breathless and typically Millwall frustrating high. The season was only half way through and we'd already been put through every emotion possible. We'd battered teams and been battered, reached the dizzy heights of automatic promotion paces, jostled among the places of the dreaded new-fangled end-of-season play-offs and envisaged what it would be like playing a winner-takes-all promotion knock-out with whoever we'd face if we finished fifth, fourth or agonisingly third. Finally, as Big Ben tolled to turn 1987 into 1988, we found ourselves in fifth place, looking forward to New Year's Day at The Den and a chance to avenge that 1-0 defeat at Leicester back in August.

It was also time to start looking towards the end of the season, warily totting up which points could possibly be gleaned from each game; who would stay the course as promotion rivals, who would fall by the wayside. Now was the time to wonder where the six-pointers would be contested and how it would all pan out over the next four months.

I had a vision, a teenage football fan's fantasy. In fact, probably a common fantasy shared by every Millwall fan at the time: a promotion party at The Den on May 7th, players doing a lap of honour, holding the Division Two Championship trophy aloft, with the strains of Queen's 'We Are The Champions' distorting the stadium's antiquated old PA speakers. To fulfil such a fantasy, a party both before and after the final match of the season at home to Blackburn, the title, not just promotion, but top spot itself, would have to be clinched at the previous match: Away to Hull on May Bank Holiday Monday, May 2nd.

I shared this dream with Dad as midnight drew closer:

"Just imagine Dad, next year, if we can clinch the title at Hull and then have a bloody great big party at The Den for the last game?" Dad looked at me as if I was mad.

"Hull? We NEVER win there..."

9
CLOCKING THE BIG GUNS

When captain Les Briley gave us a third minute lead in the New Year's Day home game against Leicester at The Den, it was enough to stun the most hungover of fans into sobriety. New Year's Day games can be a real ordeal. Twelve months earlier our new year had begun queuing outside Brighton's Goldstone Ground for a midday kick-off. The air was thick with the stench of stale alcohol, many of our number had travelled directly from their New Year's Eve sessions, and the brisk south coast wind blew the driving rain into our faces which, in freezing temperatures, felt like sandpaper rubbing our cheeks. We were made to wait for the turnstiles to open but there was little urgency as we were merely queueing to stand on The Goldstone's wide open corner away terrace which was even more exposed than the little side streets we were decamped in.

"No umbrellas are allowed in the stadium" announced an irritatingly chirpy WPC.

This was a clever tactic by her male colleagues, in that hearing that your only source of shelter was to be confiscated from a woman made it a little harder to complain. When asked what they were supposed to do with them, she replied that they could be stashed in the bushes of the park opposite the stand. Needless to say very few brollies were retrieved on the way out but ludicrously, if you are going to use an umbrella as some sort of weapon of hooliganism, it's more likely to happen after the match when you're messing about in the bushes retrieving it while the home fans stroll past you rather than on a terrace filled with your own fans separated from your rival supporters by a fifteen foot high fence. Thankfully we'd won 1-0 that day, a repeat on the first day of 1988 would set us up nicely.

After the trauma of our Barnsley battering just weeks before, we had smashed eight goals in just over two matches. Even though the expected slaughter didn't materialise, the feeling that filled the air as we left the ground that afternoon after one of the most one-sided one-nils we had ever witnessed was one of a new-found invincibility about this team – even without Cascarino. That said, the talismanic striker was now back and due to start our next match away to Ipswich just 24 hours later.

Not that we needed him at the time. That Les Briley goal was his third in consecutive matches. Briley was a perfect fit for Millwall. He had arrived in 1984, one of George Graham's finds. His footballing CV wasn't that impressive, counting Hereford, Wimbledon and Aldershot as his teams since being released by Chelsea. He didn't even look like a footballer really. A bit short, stumpy, awkward even, with a mop of hair which gave him a bit of a roguish look. But once the match started he dominated proceedings from the centre of the park like a machine. Breaking up play and moving the ball quickly, turning defence into attack and never shirking a tackle – which obviously endeared him to the Millwall crowd almost immediately and made him obvious choice as club captain. When Terry Hurlock arrived, the pair made a perfect partnership and must have been an absolute nightmare to play against. In an interview, Briley described what it was like to play for Millwall:

"At every club you play for, you believe your heart is in that club. As a professional footballer, you have to believe that. But when I came to Millwall, I realised everywhere else had just been a job."

"The place is so homely, so warm. Footballers tend to form cliques; it's one of those things."

"But here, there is a warmth between people, regardless of what they do. It's a togetherness I don't think you could get in many clubs. The people you see who don't matter, do matter, at Millwall. The groundsman, the people who sweep the terraces, the people in the offices; they really matter."

Any footballer who signs for Millwall with the attitude that it's 'just another club' and merely part of their job has never lasted long. Those that take the club, its fans and its unique culture to their hearts, the way Briley did, thrive and are afforded the luxury of being allowed to make mistakes and their limitations are accepted all the time they are giving everything.

Most of Millwall's greatest playing legends aren't necessarily the ones that have scored the most spectacular or significant goals, or possessed the greatest skill or ability, but the ones that proved week in week out, from kick-off until final whistle, playing for Millwall was the most important thing in their lives – just as supporting the team from the terraces was for the fans. It's a culture that the modern day game is sadly lacking as clubs become businesses, supporters customers and players commodities.

Such is the madness of festive English football, winning three games in five days had set us back into the top four. Equally as mad was that, in the remaining 30 days of the month, we'd only have two more league games to play.

I set off for Ipswich full of confidence – which is of course the first mistake any football fan makes. When the football special pulled in to the station and we poured off the train, it was a refreshing surprise to be able to amble through a pleasant town without the close attention of a police escort. The whole occasion had the air of a school half term holiday day out that your parents dragged you on; harmless enough, a bit dull, but a nice change from the grim, dark northern outposts rubbing shoulders with miserable Mr Plod.

The terrace behind the goal at Ipswich's Portman Road ground housed both home and away fans. It was split down the middle by a simple metal fence with a handful of Policemen scattered at various points from top to bottom either side. This sort of segregation is always fun. Being almost touching distance from the opposition fans and actually making eye contact with them after various incidents throughout the game adds to the delicious anticipation of seeing your team score a goal – and makes the dread of conceding all the greater.

After over an hour of pretty much nothing happening, the game exploded into life when a goal from Ipswich's Mich D'Avary set the locals stood next to us giddy. As they bounced up and down poking v-signs and middle fingers through the fence, half of us attempted to ignore them while the other half retaliated with a few choice insults, which was punctuated by the occasional 'ping' of a coin hitting the fence thrown from one side and then being returned.

I've never seen the point of throwing coins. Even in the school playground when I'd watched kids squander their dinner money in games of 'penny up the wall' which always escalated to 20p, 50p and the one pound up the wall and eventually 'five coin throw' where you'd chuck a variety of coins into the fray along with the other boy and call heads or tails and collect each coin that landed on the side you called. Some kids would literally go all week without food thanks to their losses.

Chucking them at football seemed even more pointless. They always seemed to ping back off the fence separating the thrower from their target. If you stood on an empty football terrace and was offered £10,000 if you could hit a one inch thick metal fence bar from ten feet away with half a dozen coins, you can guarantee they'd all go straight through the bars.

More to the point, although I was obviously annoyed that we were losing, and the gloating Ipswich lads stood just a few feet away from me mad me even madder, I wasn't mad enough to want to try and take one of their eyes out.

As the game ambled to its end, a chorus of "Have we fucked up your New Year?" started up from the home fans and, delighted by the apparent genius of creating this little gem, our companions on the other side of the fence helped it grow to an annoying crescendo, complemented with more hand gestures and pointing in an attempt to pick out individual fans to direct it to.

It's beautiful moments like this that make every penny spent, every mile travelled and every single mind-numbing goal-less draw or last minute defeat endured following your team away from home worthwhile.

With the electronic scoreboard showing the magic '90' minutes and the strains of "Have we fucked up your New Year?" growing louder above the whistles from the crowd imploring the referee to blow for full time, Tony Cascarino turned and struck home the equaliser right in front of us.

Cue mayhem.

We leapt around the terrace shrieking with a mixture of elation and laughter and, after the mandatory "EIO" goal celebration, quick as a flash started our own rendition of "Have we fucked up your New Year?" aimed at the quickly departing fans in the adjacent section. It felt like so much more than a point won. It was an enjoyable last laugh before the distraction of the cup.

I can't adequately explain how differently the FA Cup was treated back in the 1980s. The final itself was as grand an occasion as any royal wedding, where entire households would come to a standstill and the only question was which channel you watched it on as the entire spectacle was played out live on both BBC1 and ITV. The third round, where the top two divisions joined those plucky lower league and non-league hopefuls, dreaming of being another Hereford, Blyth Spartans or Bournemouth was most football fans' equivalent of Christmas.

The draw itself was very different back in 1988 too. It was almost a secretive affair. In order to hear who your team was playing in the third round, you'd have to tune in to Radio Two at lunchtime on a Monday afternoon. Listening in was almost like eaves-dropping on a private gentlemen's' club meeting. The draw would be announced by one of the suits at The Football Association, with all the ceremony of a state funeral. The unmistakable sound of the balls being shaken in their velvet bags crackled over the wireless to expectant ears.

Obviously being at school meant this event was missed every time, leaving you to find out later on in news bulletins, local papers or good old Teletext. Luckily though, on this occasion, having double Art immediately before lunch enabled us to listen in. Mr Burns, the head of the Art Department at our school had a cosy little office and in it, an antiquated old radiogram. Once we had reached the responsible level of the fifth year, he sometimes allowed us to listen to the radio. Unfortunately, the amount of stations you could find were extremely limited.

On this occasion Mr Burns had decided to listen to the radio himself and it was just as I was packing up to leave for lunch that I heard something that stopped me in my tracks:

"After the news we have the draw for the FA Cup Third Round from the Football Association at Lancaster Gate…" the announcer droned, almost like a declaration of World War Three.

"Is it OK if I stay and listen to this?" I enquired to a non-plussed Mr Burns who had no interest in football whatsoever.

He agreed and then looked on even more puzzled as I shot out of the door.

Ten minutes later the tiny office was bursting at the seams with jostling, chattering bodies, spilling into the Art Department outside. Mr Burns had fortunately long since escaped to the sanctuary of the staffroom otherwise I was certain he would have sent us all packing, not grasping the importance of this broadcasting occasion. I had dashed around the fifth year common room, disturbing the games of cards and paper-reading which had started among the various male students in my year, announcing that they could hear the cup draw and, like the Pied Piper I set off back to the art room pursued by an excited gang of football fans.

Now they assembled, eagerly awaiting the start of the draw. Fans of Palace, Chelsea, Arsenal, the token glory-hunting Liverpool supporters who had never been farther north than Liverpool Street train station and Millwall's representatives which numbered two: me and a lad called Lloyd.

As the self-important dinosaurs of the FA made their way painfully slowly through the process, excited shouts discussing their team's draw were shushed as another relevant numbered ball was drawn out and announced.

Millwall had never enjoyed good cup draws against big teams. With the exception of League and FA Cup ties against Chelsea back in 1984-85, the golden ties against the likes of Liverpool and Arsenal – two huge names in the game that we had never played at league level - eluded us. Chelsea was OK, but we had played them in the league in 1977. Spurs was also OK but again, a league fixture just a decade before. Even Manchester United were visitors to The Den in the seventies. What we really wanted was Arsenal or Liverpool.

Then it came:

"Number two"

"Arsenal"

"Will play number twenty three"

"Millwall"

The shout of "YES" from the one Arsenal fan and two Millwall supporters in the room drowned out any cheer that had gone before and rendered the rest of the draw impossible to follow.

The month-long wait for Millwall's first ever trip to Highbury to face

Arsenal was one of the biggest media circuses I can ever remember surrounding Millwall. Straight away the press picked up on the undoubted mayhem that Millwall's notorious fans would create on their day out at their illustrious neighbours and produced works of fictional fantasy on their pages that any best-selling author would be proud of. The fact that ex-Millwall manager George Graham was now in charge of The Gunners only added more spice to an already piping hot recipe. At its absolute peak of absurdity, the Daily Mirror announced with a suitably glib Cockney cliché that bets were changing hands "up and down the Old Kent Road" to steal the famous clock from the Arsenal stadium.

Gleefully dragging out details of the Luton riot three years previously, they explained, straight-faced, that "A crazy SAS-styled gang of fans from hooligan-riddled Millwall are aiming to attack and carry off Arsenal's famous clock from Highbury."

They didn't explain exactly how this special forces-style operation was going to be undertaken – whether it was to be under cover of darkness before the big day with the clock, probably weighing in at about the same rate as a small car being carried through the tight terraced streets surrounding the stadium before wedging it onto the tube and back "Across the river…" or if it was to be an even more daring raid in broad daylight in front of over 40,000 fans, television cameras and legions of the Metropolitan Police's finest.

The reality was of course nothing of the sort. Save for a few mischievous songs threatening to remove the rusty old timepiece, the crammed Clock End, which at kick off time was full to bursting up to its cordon three quarters of the way across the terrace soon creaked under the weight of 10,000 plus Lions fans, eventually resulting in the home supporters having to relinquish their place and be moved into the adjacent stand.

The crush at one point, with almost two hours to go before kick-off, was scarily uncomfortable, and I felt my rib cage being pressed harder and harder against the barrier as more fans piled in. Mercifully, there were no perimeter fences at Highbury that day and whilst fans spilling onto the pitch prompted the usual cries of "hooligans" from the nation's press the following day, it was, for the most part, nothing more than fans escaping an overcrowded enclosure.

The match itself was a non-event. Arsenal were a good side with title-winning ambitions and scored two early goals at will courtesy of Hayes and Rocastle. Gracefully they took their foot off the gas to avoid a humiliation and the match finished 2-0 to The Gunners. Whilst Millwall's performance on the day, where they appeared to choke in the face of the occasion, gave some causes for concern about our top flight credentials if we were to gain promotion that season, it was agreed that however we fared against the game's elite, we'd have a lot of fun introducing ourselves to the game's top brass.

The Millwall players had undergone the perfect initiation for their crucial next home league match against Middlesbrough who arrived at The Den seven days later in third place – one above Millwall.

Mr Green was one of three English teachers at my school. He was a decent bloke and good teacher. He certainly wasn't the sort of 'cool' teacher in the trying-to-be-your-mate, "Hi, my name's Mr Green, but you can call me Pete – hey have you heard the new record by The Smiths?" sort of way either. He was a football fan, and supported Middlesbrough. I considered myself good at spotting accents and always detected a sort of softer Geordie-style tone to his voice but it was only during this season that he revealed his roots and football colours. His two colleagues, Mr McGill and Mr Fullman were also really good teachers. They are probably the reason I took such an interest in English above all other subjects because it only seemed to be the English teachers that didn't talk to you like you was some sort of delinquent - even though many of the pupils at my school were.

Mr Green beckoned me over across a crowded common room on the Friday afternoon as I was making my way back after lunch. He explained that he was going to the Millwall v Middlesbrough match with a friend who was travelling down and was looking for some directions and the best way to the ground – and the away end of course. I scribbled a quick map and directions from New Cross Gate train station and he thanked me, apologising in advance for the three points his team were going to take off us.

As the Middlesbrough team emerged from the tunnel the cat calls and wolf whistles filled the air. If there's anything that's going to provoke a reaction from the Milllwall home crowd it's a dodgy haircut and 'Boro had them almost from one to eleven. A few seasons earlier Aston Villa had played an FA Cup replay at The Den and their winger Paul Birch, sporting a bleach blonde tight perm, was given a torrid time to the extent that his manager ending up substituting him. The burly lads from the north east would prove harder to break, but their boy band style coiffures, with floppy blonde highlighted quiffs and centre partings on top and number one shaved short back and sides gave the home fans every opportunity to try and knock them off their stride.

The first half was understandably cagey, like two boxers working their way around the ring, offering token taps to their opponent's gloves, waiting to see who would blink first. Then, ten minutes into the second half, centre back Alan Walker powered a header home to make it 1-0.

When Walker was born, I've no doubt that the midwife announced his arrival into this world not by revealing him to be a boy but by holding him aloft declaring: "It's a centre half!" The man was made to play at the back. A true warrior, he had experienced more than his fair share of drama in the game – and not always on the pitch. Three years earlier he had been in the ill-fated main stand at Valley Parade which burned to the ground claiming the lives of 56 fans. He was a Lincoln player at the time and sitting the game out through suspension. Literally weeks later, after signing for Millwall, he was crushed between goalkeeper and striker defending against a Coventry attack in a pre-season friendly at The Den and sustained a punctured lung and broken ribs. You could say it was character building.

His bullet headers from corners had become something of a trademark and Middlesbrough, clearly with the initial brief of leaving south east London with a point to keep them in third place, were sparked immediately into action, Bernie Slaven equalised within three minutes and, far from parking the Boro bus, they went all out for a priceless winner.

Surviving the onslaught, Millwall composed themselves and settled back into their rhythm, and just when it seemed that time was running out and the rare patience of the Den faithful had been in vain, up popped Teddy Sheringham to win it in the 88th minute. I found Mr Green back in the common room on Monday morning. He accepted that the best team won, and that he'd been to lots of grounds but never one as intimidating as The Den. He complimented me on my map and said that his friend, who was a cartographer, was very impressed. I didn't know what a cartographer was, but didn't like to ask. That's the only problem with English teachers, they love to slip big words into conversation knowing full well you don't know what they mean. I'd need to look that one up.

Inexplicably, it would be three weeks before Millwall had the chance to play for more valuable promotion points and the third place that they had worked so hard for against Middlesbrough would soon turned into fifth again as the rest of the month was sat out frustratingly. What they desperately needed was a run, a string of results to catapult them into a position to attack those all-important promotion places on the home straight. They were about to get it, but not before things went horribly wrong again.

Waiting for Bradford at home on the first Saturday of February felt like enduring the close season all over again. There had been the distraction of another Simod Cup tie, which had the empty atmosphere and lack of importance of one of those pre-season friendlies which reinforces the hell of the hiatus. A 3-2 defeat at home to Norwich saw us exit this most ridiculous of competitions, but then, when Bradford arrived at The Den, we found ourselves inadvertently smack bang in the middle of another one.

1988 was the centenary of The Football League. Among the many scatty sideshows the football authorities had organised to celebrate it, they'd had the ridiculous idea of a 16 team two day tournament at Wembley, cancelling all league fixtures smack bang in the middle of April – when the entire country was preparing itself for the vital home straight of the season.

The 16 teams were decided by totting up league records from the 15 matches played from November 1st. The top eight from the First Division, four from Division Two and two from Divisions Three and Four would all go to Wembley and their fans would share the crumbling old stadium which would be somehow suitably cordoned off to accommodate them all.

Going into the game with Bradford, Millwall not only faced yet another promotion rival, but were in with a chance of a first appearance at Wembley by virtue of clinging on to the fourth Centenary Tournament qualifying place – a point clear of Leeds with 14 matches played. Victory would not only give them some breathing space in fifth place over sixth placed Bradford, but give the long-suffering fans a day out at Wembley.

Just like Bournemouth at home back in November when that Wembley circus totting-up process began, things just didn't go right from the moment the match kicked off until Bradford's unnervingly lanky young substitute striker Ian Ormondroyd scuffed a last minute winner for the only goal of the game. To compound our misery, Leeds won to make it a double for Yorkshire that day.

Three days later we travelled to Birmingham and surrendered to yet another gut-wrenching late 1-0 defeat. By some miracle, these two defeats had no impact on Millwall's league position but, even though they were still nicely placed in fifth, the morale of both team and fans looked to be on a decidedly downward turn.

I'd arranged to go to our next match – Reading away – with Lloyd, the only other Millwall supporter I knew of at my school. I'd gone into a sort of numbed autopilot now, and was just determined to go to as many games as

I could afford whatever the outcome. All hope and expectation was shelved, it was too painful to manage. Little did I know that this was the very initiation of becoming a football fan and certainly not unique to me, or my team. At the time it felt as though Millwall were playing with my emotions, waiting until I had accepted that it wasn't to be our season after all following a couple of bad results, then lifting me back up again with a stellar performance. It was only February, and just a few wins would see us right back in contention for a top two place, but I decided it was best to assume the worst, take every goal and point as a bonus and just enjoy it. I was so close to getting off on the misery I almost bought a Smiths record. I suppose this is how teenage kids become goths and EMOs. I did the same, just through Millwall. It was a strangely calming feeling, freeing myself of the stress of whether we'd go up this season or not. For now it didn't really matter, not in the great scheme of things, I was in it for the long haul.

It was something of an epiphany I guess, similar but not as exhilarating to the one I experienced five years earlier when my dad took me to Millwall's last home game of the season against Brentford. Until then I hadn't really taken much notice of all the peripheral stuff that went with a football match. I watched the action of course, but often found myself drifting off bored if the game was dull and started mucking about with the other kids at the foot of the Cold Blow Lane terrace. We'd strike up impromptu games of our own using screwed up bags of Percy Dalton's Peanuts for footballs. The 82-83 season however was the first time I really took an interest in league tables. The season had started in a similar way to the 87-88 campaign. Millwall - then in the Third Division - had invested heavily in new players to win promotion. Dad was excited, which took some doing for such a cynical long-suffering old Lions fan. We arrived for the first home match of the season with great anticipation and watched open-mouthed as Cardiff battered us 4-0.

By the time May had arrived we were clinging on to our Third Division place by the skin of our teeth – needing maximum points from our last two games to stay up. A season that had got me interested in the workings of the league tables because I thought I'd be following us at the top end of the table was ending with me fixated with our rivals' run-ins at the bottom.

That final home game against Brentford was my first real taste of a big game atmosphere at The Den. It was electric from start to finish. At one point a fight broke out between the players, started by Brentford's hulking midfielder Terry Hurlock which only served to stoke the crowd up even more. The celebrations that greeted the Millwall match-winning goal and final whistle stayed with me for ages afterwards, further cementing my love for The Lions on a whole new level.

Before the game I had met up with Steve again in our usual place between the fence that divided the Cold Blow Lane terrace and halfway line. He was telling me about the previous week's match away to Reading that his dad had taken him to where Millwall had found themselves 3-0 down and reduced to nine men but fought back to 3-3 and almost won it. In one afternoon I'd gone from just following my dad to the match and playing around at the foot of the terrace to wanting to be at every game home and away, stood in the middle of the noisiest section of Millwall fans, cheering my team on.

The following week Millwall completed a remarkable relegation escape act with a 1-0 win at Chesterfield where apparently the travelling Lions fans turned the match into a virtual home game. I listened to the radio updates with Dad, desperate to be there.

I thought about the 3-3 match at Reading that Steve told me about while I stared out of the window of the football special as it pulled out of Paddington station and as the rain lashed the unwashed window of our antiquated carriage I remembered Dad's advice on Reading away, and for once it wasn't the usual "the never win there...".

"It always pisses down at Reading" he said, without looking up from his paper when I announced I was going earlier in the week.

Funnily enough, one of the details that made that epic 3-3 comeback even more dramatic according to Steve was the incessant heavy rain which at one point looked like it might threaten the game altogether.

Steve passed up the invitation to come with me that day, every spare penny he had was now being sunk into driving lessons and buying his first car. Everything he owned was flogged in pursuit of a blue Ford Capri he had his eye on, and the freedom of a driving licence.

Sure enough, the rain came down even heavier as we were marched from our train through the non-descript streets of Reading to their compact little Elm Park ground, complete of course, with fully open away terrace.

Reading took the lead after about 20 minutes and there was nothing in Millwall's play that suggested they weren't heading for a third defeat in a row and mid-table obscurity. Even a blockbusting equaliser from the same Terry Hurlock whose fighting spirit for the opposition had help light up that Brentford match five years before couldn't take our minds off the soaking we were getting as Reading quickly retook the lead and sent us in at half time 2-1 down.

As the rain trickled down the back of my coat collar while I tried to guide a hot dog dribbling in too much ketchup and mustard into my mouth with one hand – the other left thrust inside my pocket in an attempt to keep at least one part of my body reasonably warm and dry – I ignored the half time scores being broadcast over the public address as being irrelevant now to our lost cause.

I wondered instead what I might be doing now, or later that Saturday evening instead of being soaked to my skin in the middle of Berkshire or sat on a freezing cold train going home after watching another defeat. When I arrived home from school the previous day I found a couple of Valentines cards. I knew who they were from. One girl I wasn't really interested in, the other a bit more intriguing. She was a pretty blonde girl in my year called Cheryl, but she didn't just have looks, she was into football.

Any girlfriends I had up until that point usually bit the dust in a matter of weeks because I always put football – or more precisely Millwall – before them. The usual ultimatum of: "It's me or Millwall, what's it to be?" was always met with the obvious response: Millwall every time.

Cheryl was a Palace fan. Yes, I know, 'cavorting with the enemy?' I hear you cry disgusted, but that was part of the fascination if I'm honest. In his book 'Fever Pitch' Nick Hornby told about how he always thought that a fellow Arsenal fan would make the ideal life partner. When he found one, at first this was proved to be correct, but it soon turned sour. It got to a stage where they were virtually competing over who was more hurt by a defeat, or who had the best knowledge of the club's history and was therefore the bigger fan.

I quite liked the idea of going out with someone who understood why I was so mad about football, but I didn't want them at Millwall matches. That was mine, all mine. There was an agreement among us in our little group at The Den: "You don't bring your bird to the match". Steve proposed the motion and we all passed it unanimously.

The thing is, Cheryl wasn't just a Palace fan, she worked for them, in the club shop. She didn't just follow the team because she liked Neil Redfearn's legs, she actually knew about football. Because of this we'd struck up a friendly rivalry at school but, being the naïve soul that I was I never saw it as anything more than that. Until the Valentines card arrived – complete with her phone number.

I called her and suggested we go out on Sunday. A little puzzled at first, she asked why Saturday wasn't possible. She got a two word reply, and understood immediately:

"Reading away"

If I'm totally honest, a tiny little bit of me, right at the back of my head, the smallest voice, suggested that I may have made the wrong decision, but I shook this out of my conscience as quickly as it had arrived. I tipped my luke-warm rain-diluted tea onto the concrete steps below me, crumpled the polystyrene cup into the soggy sauce and mustard-soaked hot dog tissue and tossed them away as the roar went up from the Millwall fans greeting their heroes for the second half.

Six minutes later, two quick goals from Sheringham sent delirious soggy bodies bouncing around the away terrace celebrating a 3-2 win.

Would I rather be anywhere else? Of course not.

For a couple of weeks, seeing Cheryl was good fun. Being 15, we couldn't exactly go out on the lash at the Gin Palace, but the football chat made a change from the usual awkward stuff, the uncomfortable silences, you know the thing. It was mainly trips to the cinema or playing cards with her folks, who were also good fun, but loved to wind me up, and the first time I met them, they had fairly good reason.

Apparently, one of the players had called an unofficial team meeting on the coach during the journey to Reading. A few home truths were told and the team resolved to pick themselves up and give everything for the remaining 13 games of the season, that was certainly in evidence during the second half at Reading, now we needed to back it up by beating mid-table Oldham at home a week later. It should have been a formality. It wasn't of course, and I'm convinced I jinxed it. Thursday nights were a favourite of mine. Fish and chips for dinner, Top of the Pops on the box and of course, that little bit closer to the weekend. Thursday night was also Pools night. Dad would sit and carefully mark his ten little Xs in the boxes for his 'eight from ten' entry and then pray that the dividends would be favourable that weekend and he'd scoop the £850,000 top prize then hand in his notice on Monday morning. It was the National Lottery of its day, millions of dreams, destined never to be fulfilled.

I used to take an interest in the opposite side of the coupon, where you just had to predict home or away wins, which seemed a lot easier to me. While

Dad was still finishing off his dinner, I glanced at the weekend's fixtures and decided to give it a go. I quickly selected what I thought to be seven or eight home bankers, took a punt on one more and then pondered my last choice. Nothing was screaming out at me, apart from one, but I couldn't choose that one. Could I?

My pen hovered over 'Millwall v Oldham'. We had to beat them didn't we? Of course we did. The trouble was, as everyone knows, betting on your own team is the best way to guarantee they'll cock it up. Now I had another problem. I had already thought about choosing Millwall to win at home. You can guarantee that, if I bottled out and didn't mark them down to win, they would, and the match I chose instead would let me down. If I did choose Millwall to win, they would of course blow it, and the other nine would come it. Abandoning my superstitions for a split second, I scrawled my X next to Millwall v Oldham, plopped my pound coin bet on top of Dad's neat little pile of coins for his entry and handed it all over to the Pools man when he came to collect the coupon later that evening.

For fourteen glorious minutes I thought the fates were finally on my side. What looked like a coupon-busting 0-0 draw all over for one hour suddenly sparked into life when Cascarino rolled the ball home to give Millwall the lead. All we had to do was hold on, or preferably put the game to bed with a couple more goals. As the game ambled into the last ten minutes, Millwall seemed to have given up bothering and Oldham made an almost token foray into the Millwall half. Then, out of nowhere, they scored. The second I saw the ball nestle in the back of Brian Horne's net, I knew. I hadn't heard any half time or latest scores from my other nine selections, but I was as certain as I could be of anything that this was going to finish 1-1 and be the one and only game in ten that I hadn't correctly predicted. Which of course it was.

As I flicked through the final scores on teletext soon after arriving home, I checked off each and every one of the other nine correctly predicted home wins.

Then, like a fool, I related the whole sorry episode to Cheryl and her Palace-mad mum and dad when I visited them that evening. It was at this point that I started to doubt the whole 'date a rival team's fan' thing, especially as we were playing Palace at home in three weeks.

I was learning the hard way this season about the things that didn't mix with football: Religion, Gambling and Women.

As you've probably gathered, my dad wasn't the sort of father that would devote hours of his spare time kicking a ball about with me or helping me with my Airfix models. If he wasn't out at work, he was doing something on the house: fixing, replacing, tidying, digging the garden over and then, after all that, resting. I got the odd bedtime story as a very young boy, and he'd take me along with him to the newsagent on a Sunday morning to get his paper and then, if the weather was decent, on to Clapham Common where he'd try and hunt down some of his old mates who were still playing Sunday morning football. I'd be left to my own devices, messing about on the bandstand, watching the old blokes playing chess, or the big kids with their remote control boats on the lake. As far as Dad knew, I wasn't even there.

That changed a little when he took me to my first Millwall match. He seemed surprised that I had enjoyed it so much and wanted to go again. It was more of a pleasant shock to his cynical old system that I behaved myself too. Selfishly at first, he saw it as a way to get his regular fix of Millwall without getting earache off my mum for her having to put up with me under her feet. As I got older, it became a firm bond between us, but sadly the only one.

We didn't share anything else in common. He could be a bit of a cold fish at times. He felt the pressures of struggling to pay the bills through the seventies when he was made redundant several times, the ignominy of applying for a rent rebate at our Balham council flat and the pain of not owning his own home. I can remember very vividly, in the days when he was out of work (it was at the same time that I was just starting school) him rising at six and having his usual strip wash and shave in the bathroom, then putting on his grey suit and leaving our flat to look for work, not returning until at least six that evening having spent the day chasing every job that the local Labour Exchange threw at him.

He was from a generation that didn't privately shower their young with love and affection, and certainly weren't prone to great outward displays of it either. He did his fair share of the household chores but was obsessed with tidiness and the first thing he'd do on arriving home from work each evening was pop his head around the door to the front room where I'd invariably be playing or watching television, to check that the room was tidy. If it wasn't, he'd reserve his anger for Mum and I'd hear him shouting and moaning to her in the kitchen about how the "place looked like a pig sty".

A slight over-reaction of course, up until the age of about eleven, all my worldly goods amounted to a biscuit tin full of Matchbox cars, a carrier bag full of Action Man stuff another one full of Lego and an entry level Subbuteo set. The contents of all this was usually strewn over the front room carpet having been part of various games since I arrived home from school and thus contributed to the 'pig sty'. Dad's head would appear at the door and I felt with a slightly disappointed look as if to say: "Oh, are you still here then?", and then quickly survey the room to check it was tidy, which it rarely was. Then it was off to hang up his coat and rant at Mum. By the time he'd persuaded her to come and inspect the mess herself, I had quickly scooped the whole lot up, stacked it neatly under the table and was sat on the sofa enjoying the last throes of Ivor the Engine.

Once I'd outgrown the toy cars, Action Man and Lego adventures and most of my Subbuteo players had broken free of their bases, rendering all matches off, I was more than happy sat listening to the radio from the time I arrived home from school until Dad came home. Steve Wright in the Afternoon and the Bruno Brookes Drive time show through my headphones plugged into my trusty old Aiwa midi system was enough to keep me happy until dinner time – and Dad would be suitably impressed with the tidy room on his arrival home too. Everyone was a winner.

When I'd really caught the Millwall bug Dad's arrival home was eagerly anticipated – especially on Tuesdays and Fridays when the Millwall news in the local South London Press newspaper could be dissected. Dad seemed happier to see me too. For a man of very limited bonding skills, Millwall had provided the glue which stuck us together.

Then there was the flipside. We clashed and butted heads on pretty much every other topic you could imagine. My teenage years had given me a voice and an opinion that I was only too happy to air and this was at conflict with a dad who had been brought up to never utter a word to his own father unless spoken to first. Punishment was the same whatever the misdemeanor: the belt. At the age of about ten, my dad and his friends had been chased by the local Bobby after being caught 'scrumping' – stealing apples from a neighbour's garden apple tree. The PC had given chase as the team of miscreants leapt over the wall at the end of the garden and scarpered down the alley that ran along the back of the houses. They had been disturbed by the home owner and – as was often the risk in those days – emerged from the alley into the main road just as the local Constable was walking his beat. Immediately sensing they were up to no good he gave chase but was thwarted as they scattered in different directions. Dad had got away with it. Or so he thought. The pursuit had been brief, but long enough for the Policeman to recognise the faces. By the time my dad arrived home, his dad had already been visited and filled in with all the details of the crime. No action would be taken, that would be left to Dad's dad.

I can remember him telling me the story of how he knew, the minute his dad opened the door to him that evening, that the game was up and retribution was imminent. His dad stood there holding the door in his left hand and his large leather belt in the right. Moments later it was lashed across Dad's backside with little attempt to save him the extra pain of the heavy metal buckle. He confessed to me that the pain and fear was such that he actually wet himself – which in turn earned him a smack around the head from his mum as he gingerly removed his clothes.

I hated that story, and felt so sorry for my younger dad. It only made me wonder all the more why, despite this harsh upbringing, he worshipped the ground his dad walked on and dutifully nursed him to his death after he suffered a stroke four years before I was born, meaning I'd never met the man, which, if I'm honest, I was quite relieved at.

Dad would often respond to my backchat with reminders of what his dad would have done to him "if he'd spoken to him like that". This only served to escalate matters when I would dismiss such behaviour – and the granddad that I never met – as a headcase, or a psycho, leading Dad to then defend the man who beat him with a heavy belt. Voices would raise, Mum would try to intervene and almost always end up in tears with me leaving the house, slamming the door behind me as Dad continued shouting over Mum's sobs.

The problem really started when I was eleven. I'd just started high school which was character-building to say the least. My mum had found a lump in her breast and the doctor wanted her to have it removed as soon as possible to rule out cancer. Of course I wasn't party to the details, just the fact that mum had found a lump and was going into hospital for a few days to have it removed. For three days, dad was in charge. On the Monday I arrived home from school to an empty house. Dad arrived home at six with fish and chips for dinner. Once this was eaten we caught the train to West Croydon before walking the mile or so down London Road to Mayday hospital to visit mum. They spoke in tense, hushed tones about stuff I couldn't hear, punctuated only by Dad tutting and shaking his head.

The train journey home was spent with Dad slumped forward with his head in his hands with me not really knowing what was going on but sensing it was pretty bad.

We repeated this process the following day. Fish and chips for dinner is great, it's a treat, but two days on the bounce suggested Dad was struggling on the domestic front. Like a lot of 1980s dads, he was clueless in the kitchen, I don't think I ever saw him so much as make a sandwich or even fill a bowl with cereal. I'm not saying my palette was too sophisticated to stomach a hat-trick of battered haddock but I really couldn't face the prospect if a third consecutive meal eaten off greasy paper. After our second silent train journey home I told him that I'd sort our evening meal the next day and he simply nodded.

When he arrived home on Wednesday evening I had managed to boil up some frozen peas and throw together some instant mash and a couple of pies that were in the freezer. I doubt my low-budget pie and mash was any more nutritious than Monday or Tuesday's offering but to me it was important that we sat and ate a home-prepared meal on plates, with knives and forks. We made our final trip to the hospital to visit Mum. She was discharged the next day and her tests results later revealed that the lump was harmless.

Mum was fine, but I'd watched Dad quickly unravel in front of my eyes at the slightest hint of crisis rather than step up and look after his eleven-year-old son. Until that week I used to fret about something happening to my dad and worry about how just me and Mum would cope because he always seemed to be the driving force that ran our little family unit. After that week I saw him differently. Of course I couldn't possibly have known the deep-seated reasons why he reacted so badly to the prospect of Mum being seriously ill, I just took it all at face value, and lost a large chunk of respect for my dad, even though things were quickly back to normal again.

I loved to listen to his old Millwall stories, and he was happy to repeat them over and over at my request. My favourite one was of the 1971-72 season – the only time previously that Millwall had come close to gaining promotion to the top flight. Dad always told the story like a mini romance, a tale of two working class people coming together and how it intertwined with a tragic football tale. To me it was like one of those 'Play For Today' dramas the BBC used to show in the 70s:

In the July of 1971 my mum and dad were married, weeks later she found out she was pregnant with me. Dad was, as usual, a regular at Millwall, and getting to as many away games as he could afford. The team were looking a good bet for promotion and for most of the season occupied one of the top two promotion places. In 1972 there were no play-offs, only the champions and runners- up got the spoils. Norwich were the strong contenders and would tighten their hold on top spot as the season neared its end. There were only ever two other teams in it: Millwall and Birmingham. Dad was delicately balancing his time between working long hours as a labourer, looking after his pregnant newly-wed wife and following his football team.

With two games left and my mum ready to drop, my dad was gearing himself up for an eventful May, celebrating his beloved Lions getting promoted to the promised land of the First Division for the first time in their history, and becoming a dad.

Millwall went into their last game of the season at home to Preston having lost their advantage over Birmingham. But still in with a chance of clinching promotion. Preston were beaten easily and all they needed now was a Birmingham loss at Sheffield Wednesday to seal promotion. As the final whistle blew fans spilled onto the pitch in celebration after word had spread that Birmingham had slipped up. Realising that these terrace Chinese whispers had prompted a full-on promotion party that some of the players seemed to be starting to believe and join in, the stadium announcer burst the bubble by announcing that Birmingham had won. Millwall had completed their 42 games for the season and finished second, a point ahead of Birmingham. But Brum had a game left, away to Orient, which they duly won, and stole second place a few days later.

A week or so after this, I was born apparently, but that didn't seem to figure too prominently in the narrative.

Dad said the club never recovered from that devastating blow. To come so close and have promotion seemingly snatched away from them was too much to bear for players and fans alike. The team broke up and two seasons later dropped into the Third Division – just as the Football League decided to change the rules and allow the third placed team to gain promotion!

Dad would always finish this story with the same solemn statement:

"That's the closest they've ever been to the First Division, I won't live to see them there now…"

Experts say that nine is the age at which most children first confront the concept of death, and with it, the loss of their parents. For me it was a few years younger. My maternal grandmother lived with us in our flat in Balham. It was an old-fashioned set-up where one generation looked after the other at the family home. When I was three, she fell and broke her hip walking to her bedroom. She died a few days later in hospital, just a few days before Christmas. It was the reason my mum hated the festive season, and she always reminded me of that each year I started to get excited about the most wonderful time of the year, which detracted from the enjoyment somewhat, but was understandable for her.

I remember the empty feeling of the house after she had gone and it didn't take too much working out – even for my young mind – how much worse that could be if the same happened to my mum, dad or both.

I loved hearing that 1971-72 season story, but the last line always upset me. As shaky as my relationship was with my dad, I obviously hated the thought of him not being around and wanted, more than anything, not only to see Millwall in the First Division, but to see them there with Dad at my side on the terraces at The Den.

It only served to add even more significance to the final few matches of the season.

10
MEET THE PARENTS

As the season quickly turned towards its home straight, I finally hung up my own boots. It all ended very suddenly and with a bizarre sense of symmetry. I was playing my third successive season at the same team, which was almost unheard of for me. I was of average ability. My lack of confidence held me back more than my prowess with a ball to be honest. I was one of those players that excelled in training matches or five-a-sides but struggled to get into games when the serious stuff kicked off. I enjoyed it, that was the main thing, and the team I was in was run by a really decent bloke called Danny – the absolute opposite of Splodgegun – a man who ran the team to allow his son and other football-mad lads to enjoy playing football.

The club was called Alpha FC – we used to joke they called it that so they could be top of the league for at least one week per year – before any games had been played and the teams were listed in alphabetical order. I'd answered an appeal in our local paper which said that the local team were looking for players for its under 13s. The main problem being that I was at under 14 age level.

Undeterred, I felt this was an opportunity to gain some confidence in a match environment. Surely as an under 14 playing in an under 13 league it'd be a doddle? I called the number and spoke to Danny – whose voice instantly reminded me of Jimmy Greaves. I attended the first trials only to discover I was the only potential new recruit. The squad appeared to be a bit of a rag-tag bunch who messed about – and all of whom were visibly shorter than me.

"You're a tall lad aren't you?" was Danny's instant reaction as I introduced myself. I'd had a bit of a growth spurt at the time and it was agreed by family members at Christmas get-togethers that I'd probably end up being "a six-footer" like my uncle George and not a five-and-a-half-foot "short-house" like my dad, his brother, his own dad and other uncles. They were wrong. I'm the same five feet nine now that I was back then.

Within minutes of the practice match being set up I'd scored a couple of headed goals from corners. Danny said he'd be round to my house with the paperwork for me to sign up for the 85-86 season, he'd just need my parent's signature, two passport photos and to see my birth certificate.

True to his word, Danny called at my house one evening the following week and my dad invited him in. They chatted away about football and we signed the various forms. The distraction of my dad's chat seemed to have side-tracked any mention of the birth certificate – until I was seeing Danny out of the door.

"Oh, sorry, I almost forgot, I just need to see your birth certificate…" he said as I was about to shut the door, thinking I'd pulled it off.

"Ah, yes", I stammered, "we're having trouble finding it, can I bring it along to the next training session?"

Danny looked a little perplexed for a second but smiled kindly and said: "Yeah of course". Obviously Danny never got to see my birth certificate. I pleaded with my dad to come and watch my first game. It was a Surrey County Cup match at home to a team called Oxshott Colts. By amazing good fortune, our home games were played at the local Ashburton High School – a ten minute walk from our house. Dad somewhat reluctantly agreed to come along.

I felt unusually confident. Being a year older and a few inches taller than everyone else certainly helped and, complete with my single 'lucky' Millwall sweatband (I only wore one, it was my own take on a footballing fashion led by Aston Villa's Peter Withe a few years earlier) I was well and truly in the zone. I used to love the odd looks that sweatband got from opposition players. Within minutes of kick-off we were awarded a corner, the ball was floated across from the right and I crashed it into the top left corner with a bullet header.

I instantly turned to find Dad on the touchline alongside the other parents who were applauding my goal but he was nowhere to be seen. About ten minutes later my fellow striker, a really good player by the name of Andy, unselfishly squared the ball to me when he only had the keeper to beat and I stroked the ball in the net to make it two. I wheeled away to celebrate, but still no Dad.

As half time came with us 2-0 to the good, I saw the unmistakable figures of my parents ambling over from the school field gates. Apparently Mum had decided to join Dad but, as mums tend to do, had taken her own sweet time getting ready with no thought whatsoever for such details as kick-off times.

The fact that they had missed my goals seemed completely lost on them and when Oxshott scored four without reply in the second half their attentions inexplicably turned to the Under 9s who were playing on the adjacent pitch. To my utter disdain, all they could talk about on the walk home was how "cute the littl'uns were".

Dad did manage to take in a few Alpha matches from the kick off, but his enthusiasm levels never matched that of the other parents and he quickly stopped altogether, but I wasn't too bothered. Our early season promise in 87-88 had tailed off alarmingly when the three best players we had were poached by rival teams and we hurtled down the league.

The final straw came in an early Spring match away to Carshalton Juniors – a well organised team full of up-coming prospects for the club's semi-pro non-league team. They battered us 33-0 – the exact same score that I suffered in my first ever junior match for Norwood United some six seasons earlier and after the match Danny decided to call it a day. It was a shame, but I couldn't help feeling a little relieved that I was now able to fully focus on the version of football that was quickly consuming my life: watching Millwall and seeing us reach the First Division.

Our next two games were away, at Swindon and then Shrewsbury. Both teams were mid table and it should have been a fairly straightforward six points before the big one: Palace at home.

Us Londoners tend to be pretty uninterested about anyone or anywhere outside our own little capital city bubble. As my obsession with Millwall sent me on adventures around the country, I found it interesting to hear the opinions of my travelling companions about the places we visited. Everywhere beyond Watford was "up north" and most of our other destinations were assumed to be farming communities. So far we'd been 'up north' to the likes of Leicester, Stoke and of course Sheffield among others, and sampled the farming delights of Ipswich.

It quickly became obvious to me that the rest of the country seemed to have a bit of an unhealthy obsession with people from London. It was all "you Cockney this" and "you Cockney that" – especially from our friends in the north of course - but equally and amusingly so from the likes of Ipswich and Leicester fans and others who I never really imagined being remotely bothered about us, as we were completely oblivious to them.

I think it's possibly this total lack of recognition of anything outside London being of any importance that stoked this angst. I remember hearing our destination discussed very briefly as the supporters coach pulled away and headed for the M4:

"Swindon? What's that?"

"Farmers. Fuckin' Worzels mate."

Note the question was "what's that", not "where's that". Confirmation that we really didn't care for our destination as a place as such and once it was ascertained that it wasn't up north they were duly labelled alongside a 1970s novelty farmers pop group.

The way I've described it makes us sound very ignorant and perhaps perpetuates the tired old stereotype of Millwall fans being thick. That's not really the case here. The truth is most of the supporters that travelled all over the country knew exactly whereabouts in England their latest destination was, you don't put all those miles in season after season and not grasp a decent geographical understanding of the country you live in. The fact was they didn't care, and why should they?

My dad was a classic example of this. He had a very thorough knowledge of the specific county that any given English location was in, which he passed on to me. He had told me, a few years before when I no doubt asked him in the off-chance that it wasn't very far away and we could maybe go to a Millwall away game there that Swindon was in Wiltshire. And no, we wouldn't be going because we never win there. However, I'm sure had my dad been with me on that coach and he had been asked about our destination that day, he may well have opted for "farmers" instead of "Wiltshire" as his reply. That's just the way it was.

I on the other hand, in my 15-year-old naivety may well have offered not just the fact that Swindon was in Wiltshire, but was also the home town of XTC – one of my favourite groups. I can't imagine what the reaction to that would have been. I settled back into my seat, relieved that I hadn't been asked. Lesson learned!

Music remained my other obsession in life alongside football. I wasn't happy simply enjoying a tune. If I liked it, I had to know who sung it, what it was about and where the artist was from. I spent hours reading the NME as a six, seven and eight-year-old and barely understanding a single bloody word of it in my quest for music knowledge.

The first time I heard "Making Plans for Nigel" I thought it was the most amazing sound ever. I can remember hearing it as I walked with Dad through our estate to my first Millwall matches. Our walk took us from our own block past several others before we left the estate and made our way towards Clapham High Street train station. Residents of the Weir Road Estate were busying themselves with weekend chores which always seemed to be accompanied by a radio on a window ledge or open door. I remember that XTC track faintly emanating from someone's bathroom. The distinctive guitars and "woo oohs" escaped out of the small top window which was pegged open with its little metal rod. It stuck in my head all that weekend. Who sung it? What was it called? Luckily I was able to rely on my equally music-mad and much older cousin Glen who lived in one of the other blocks on our estate who quickly gave me the full title and band name from my amusing little rendition and Mum had her next Monday morning Woolworths order ready to go by the end of that weekend.

Swindon proved to be much less exciting than those fantastic post-punk sounds that they gave birth to. I spent a bit of a non-event of a match stood at the back of the away terrace behind the goal which overlooked local residents' back gardens, wondering if any of the members of XTC were football fans and amused myself with the thought of their lead singer Andy Partridge stood behind the goal at the end willing his team to 'beat this bunch of Cockney so-and-sos.'

An early Cascarino goal gave us a very routine 1-0 win and from the moment he nodded in after an Alan McLeary effort was saved the remaining 75 minutes or so of the game was played out almost like a pre-season friendly, which was no bad thing. Millwall were finally starting to look ruthless, well organised, getting the job done and then shutting up shop. Much of the second half was spent trying to start up conversation with the locals popping out to their back gardens below us to check if their smalls were dry yet. It was the sort of cosy little league set up that was fun, but one that we were desperate to leave behind.

Your coach would pull up at a friendly little town with a token handful of Police, park in the club car park and you would stroll up to the turnstile, pay a few quid to stand on a crumbling terrace, watch your team win in front of a sparse crowd, take the mickey out of the locals, have a few spotty kids flick you the Vs as you walked out and got back on the coach and home again. What we wanted to sample now was the big time, days out like Arsenal in the cup every other week, with huge Millwall followings and seeing what the thirty and forty thousand home fans at Old Trafford, Anfield and Goodison made of us. But for now, there was Swindon and Shrewsbury. The Shrews were fighting relegation and held us to a frustrating 0-0 draw, but I wasn't there to watch that one as, for the first time ever, I'd agreed to swap Millwall for girls. Mistake. Massive mistake.

I'd invited Cheryl to my house for the Saturday evening and we were all sat in our front room. My parents were nowhere near as sociable and chatty as Cheryl's and I was praying Dad would take Mum for a few drinks at the Cherry Trees pub as they often did, but Mum looked comfy in her chair with her magazine and Dad was engrossed in his paper as we tried to look interested in Blind Date on TV. Awkward just didn't do it justice.

I felt the time was right for a nice gesture, something to introduce Cheryl to my family, tell her a little bit of background, and lay to rest my dad's morbid prophecy. The plan was to have dad tell his little story and then, when he got to the depressing bit at the end, put a reassuring arm around him and announce that this was the year we'd see the mighty Lions promoted to the First Division, together – and at the expense of Palace. I couldn't have made a worse call if I'd tried.

"Here Dad, tell us about when you got married and I was born and Millwall missed out on promotion…"

That was my clumsy lead-in, the messy introduction that was intended to give my new girlfriend a witty insight in to me and my family. Cheryl seemed quite keen to hear the tale as Dad cleared his throat and began the old anecdote back at the church in July 1971. My mum, like most mums I guess, has that innate talent of appearing to be barely in the room at all, let alone listening to what you're saying, and then suddenly joining the conversation having taken in every word.

Dad had never told this tale in the presence of my mum, and I was about to find out why. Dad had barely got started with his little bit about how they had only been married a few weeks before my mum announced that she was pregnant, when my mum looked up from her People's Friend and said, as calmly as if asking if anyone wanted a cup of tea:

"Yeah and when I told him I was pregnant he said: 'get rid of it, we don't want a kid…'"

And with that she returned to her magazine, leaving both me and my dad open-mouthed at the revelation and poor Cheryl unsure of where to look.

Now we all know that not all pregnancies are planned, that wouldn't have been a problem, but to hear that your dad was dead set against your very existence on hearing the news that his new spouse was expecting was a shock to say the least.

To be told for the first time at the age of fifteen whilst sat next to a girl you had been going out with for a couple of weeks was the stuff of nightmares. Dad regained some semblance of composure and stuttered through the rest of the story. Cheryl looked on awkwardly.

All three of us kept glancing occasionally at Mum, waiting for her to interject with another new segment of the story about how Dad had tried to chuck her down the stairs or give her a sly kick in the guts every once in a while - which mercifully of course he didn't.

Before Dad could deliver the final heart-wrenching line, the details had been drowned out by the cheers coming from the television with Cilla announcing who James from Watford had chosen after my mum had turned up the volume having finished her reading.

I jumped up and shattered the awkwardness with a single clap of my hands and announced with all I could muster to hide my absolute humiliation:

"Right, I'll walk you home now eh Cheryl?"

She could tell I had been hurt by the whole episode and I was grateful for the diplomatic way in which she avoided ever mentioning the incident again. She was, as most teenage girls tend to be, more mature than her years and far more mature than me.

It was an episode that could have spelt trouble for my relationship with my dad. A lot of young men in my position would have seen it as the perfect opportunity to rebel. It could have turned the regular occurrences of father-son tension into pure hatred on my part and all-out war.

Fortunately – for both of us – I didn't see it that way. I could tell straight away, the moment those words left my mum's lips that Dad regretted that outburst. At the same time, he knew it was pointless trying to either deny it or play it down and it was clear that it was something that had troubled my mum since the day she revealed she was expecting and he hit back with his instant and unpleasant response.

The biggest problem was, in all of those fifteen or so years since, as far as I know, he had never tried to resolve it. I can only assume that he never took my mum to one side and told her how much he regretted saying it. For me that much is clear by the way my Mum clearly still felt so strongly about it. That was Dad all over. He was completely unable to open up about anything, not out of stubbornness, but out of the sheer inability to know where to start. Everything was kept bottled up.

So far from feeling anger towards him, I started to feel sympathy. That in turn felt uncomfortable, because at the time I felt you should only feel sorry for your parents when they become too old, ill or frail to look after themselves and rely on you to help them. Up until then, they're the ones who should be strong, set the example and call the shots. I was discovering more and more chinks in my dad's armour with every year and it was unsettling, mainly because of the fear of what I'd uncover next.

Nerves are a funny thing. I learned from a young age that the biggest fears and most debilitating nerves lie within the anticipation rather than the participation and most if the time they dissipate the second you actually get into it and confront them. Once it all kicks off they usually go out of the window.

My nerves in the build-up to Millwall v Palace began the moment I walked through the school gates on the Monday morning. By Friday I was barely able to focus on anything other than the various scenarios of that crucial clash. Defeat was unthinkable, victory almost too brilliant to contemplate for fear of never experiencing it. As John Cleese's character in the film Clockwise so perfectly put it: "It's not the despair, I can take the despair, it's the hope…"

The tension was evident more than usual as we took our places at The Den for the game. The biggest fear was to concede early, or be over run and for the game to be all over by half time. The caginess of the opening 30 minutes assured us that wouldn't be the case and Palace looked happy with a first half of containment.

Millwall started the second half with renewed energy even though we had the unfamiliar experience of watching them attack the 'wrong end' for the second half. Superstition forms a huge part of football and most clubs have a favoured end to attack each half. At Millwall, it was customary throughout generations of teams to ensure that the main home end - the Cold Blow Lane terrace – was where they would attack in the second half.

My dad would place huge importance on this and take great interest in the ritual of coin-tossing for kick-off or ends at the start of the match. Once the ref had blown and indicated that Millwall were to defend the Cold Blow Lane end in the first half, Dad would be satisfied that this particular omen had been preserved, always with the same comment which belied his usual pessimistic outlook: "Good, all the goals down this end in the second half…"

It's not as if the opposite end – the Ilderton Road terrace – was given over purely to away fans. Most of it – the large section behind the goal – was for Millwall fans, with the away supporters crammed into a tiny corner next to it. This was just the way of things, and I can hardly remember a single match that we didn't finish attacking the Cold Blow Lane end. Until that day of course.

Superstitions appeared to be put to bed nine minutes into the second half when Sheringham gave us the lead. Palace looked out of sorts, not the usual slick, swaggering side that had out-maneuvered us at their place back in October. We looked comfortable, and the only thing missing from a perfect performance was another goal or two to settle us. Even as the game moved into injury time and the whistles filled the air pleading with the referee to bring it all to an end, Palace didn't look in any way threatening. At almost five to five, it was hard to see where the extra time was coming from.

"He's waiting for them to score an equaliser" chirped Ernie, Stuart's dad. We laughed hollow laughs, unsure whether to take the comment in jest or as a gloomy premonition.

A cheer went up as Sheringham cut to the Palace by-line and in a half-hearted attempt to cross the ball, played it off a Palace defender for a corner. Surely that was it? The cheers to turned howls of disgust as both linesman and referee indicated a goal kick. Sheringham's protests fell on deaf ears and Palace sensed a break of fortune. Their fans, who until now had been silent, stirred into life as the goal kick was launched and you could almost hear them: "Imagine if we score now…"

In an instant the ball was in our 18 yard box. Palace had pace and skill with abundance in the likes of Ian Wright, Mark Bright and Andy Gray and the Millwall defence was clearly on high alert after a relatively quiet afternoon. Palace also had Jim Cannon, an aging, tight permed, moustached throwback of a footballer for whom the after-dinner circuit had been beckoning for quite some time.

This season would almost certainly be his swan-song as a Palace stalwart, one-club-man and loyal servant. As a defender Cannon was your typical seventies centre half. He was an uncompromising, row Z merchant who, in the words of Alan Hansen, 'played the percentages'. He certainly wasn't a goal threat, but for this final foray into Millwall's half, Palace had understandably thrown everyone forward.

Just as we felt the threat of Wright and Bright had been quashed by shepherding play away to the right of our goal with all other danger-men tightly marshalled, Palace somehow managed to scramble the ball across the face of the Millwall goal. At chest height it seemed harmless enough and we waited for the danger to be hoisted clear and for the referee to finally put us out of our misery. Suddenly, the ball seemed to ping down off a hand, Cannon's hand, and then onto his boot and finally into the back of the net.

That most horrible of sounds: the away fans hysterically celebrating a last minute goal, echoed around the ground for a split second before it was punctuated with boos and shouts of "Cheat, cheat cheat" aimed at the officials. Typically, the second Millwall kicked off to restart the game the referee brought the match to an end, which only served to rejuvenate the celebrations from the away end, and protests from Millwall supporters.

That evening I had to endure three hours of incessant, albeit good-natured piss-taking from Cheryl's parents. What made it worse was, for all my shouting and singing that day, I was almost too hoarse to even respond, which only made them laugh even more. I made very little effort to hide my total disdain for all things Palace and, if I'm totally honest, spent the evening sulking like a five-year-old.

On the few occasions I visited Cheryl's house, she and her parents asked me to call and let the phone ring once then hang up to let them know I had arrived home safely, which I had always done the moment I got in. On this occasion I deliberately chose not to. Hardly a great statement of defiance, but like I said, I was sulking on a level way before my 15 years.

The following Friday, Cheryl finished with me. She said she felt we 'got on better as friends'. That old chestnut, but she was right. I didn't blame her, there were three people in our short-lived relationship, and she was a very poor second behind Millwall.

I wasn't particular bothered in the great scheme of things. I'd spent the week aggravating my frazzled vocal chords by rebuffing all gloating from Palace fans at school by informing them they were a lucky bunch of ref-bribing cheats who'd get their come-uppance at the end of the season.

I didn't know how, but they would.

11
TWELVE YARDS TO GLORY

Nothing repairs hurt pride quicker than a big win. Millwall managed to get the disappointment of the Palace tragedy out of their system seven days later with a 4-1 battering of doomed Huddersfield, which also quickly helped me adjust to being single again. We should have matched the ten that Manchester City put past them earlier in the season being 2-0 up inside six minutes. The 6,000 crowd was half the attendance of the previous week's Palace clash, less a reflection on the fickleness of Millwall's support, more representative of the resignation among its long-suffering fans that this two steps forward, one step back season wasn't going to end in success.

Two weeks separated the Huddersfield win and our next match – an Easter Saturday clash with title favourites Aston Villa at The Den. We had seven games left and encouragingly for those of us who still felt promotion was a possibility, Villa were the only team we were left to face who shared upward aspirations. A tricky midweek trip to Leeds (where we "never win") was the only match that you'd imagine could pose a real threat to us taking all three points from every game potentially. 'Potentially' is of course a paradise island, a million miles west of where we dwell – in good old Reality…

Blackburn, who had gone on a record-breaking run of wins that had taken them from bottom half to chief contenders for the second remaining automatic spot had understandably ran out of steam and appeared to be limping towards the play-off finish line. There were three play-off places up for grabs. The competition was still in its infancy, having been brought in the previous season in an attempt to boost attendances, and the original format of including the team finishing fourth bottom in the First Division to fight to regain their place was used over the first two seasons of the play-offs to reduce the top flight to 20 teams. The top duo in Division Two would be promoted automatically, third place would play fourth in a two-leg semi-final, and fifth place would face the team finishing third-bottom in Division One, also over two legs, with the winners fighting it out over two games for the final top flight place.

Fighting it out might have been an appropriate choice of words. A glance at the league tables as we went into that Huddersfield match showed Millwall in the ominous fifth place and three of the teams in danger of finishing in the all-important 18th place to face them included Spurs, West Ham and Chelsea!

The fans returned in good numbers for top-of-the-table Aston Villa at home. Regardless of what they thought of Millwall's promotion credentials, they liked nothing more than the opportunity to cut a big name down to size. If we couldn't win promotion, we'd have a good laugh messing it up for someone else. In glorious sunshine, Danis Salman, fired Millwall into a 30th minute lead. Salman was one of those unlikely heroes you get at your club from time to time. Signed from manager John Docherty's old club Brentford, most fans were underwhelmed by the capture, feeling it was just a job for an old mate. But he proved himself to be the sort of player that Millwall fans love. A grafter, a roll-your-sleeves-up, get-stuck-in, no whinging, no excuses, honest full back who loved to bomb forward at every opportunity. Villa's lethal frontman Garry Thompson levelled things up right on half time – usually a sickener – but for once it didn't seem to quieten the carnival atmosphere. Within five minutes of the second half starting, Millwall were back in front courtesy of a Teddy Sheringham goal, celebrated in the now familiar fashion of scaling the Cold Blow Lane perimeter wall and saluting the celebrating throngs of fans with a shaking fist or pointed hand above the spiked railings.

The match ended 2-1 and as we walked away from the ground hearing results coming in from other games, a sudden realisation dawned on me: we were actually in with a real chance of going up. There was just one problem, four days later we travelled to Leeds. In ten previous meetings between the two clubs we had managed a win at Leeds once: in 1931, the first time we'd ever faced them.

Finding out how your rivals had fared was something of a mission back in the 1980s. The announcement of final scores over the public address system at The Den was hap-hazard to say the least, even though half time scores were usually read out with regular efficiency. There was nothing worse than hearing that a rival team was trailing at half time, wondering if they'd lost and having to wait ages to actually find out. We'd sometimes hang around in our place on the terrace expecting to hear some final scores, only to hear nothing and miss the next train home.

One sure fire routine was to follow the Radio Man. That wasn't his official nickname, it's the only way I can describe him. He was a short chap, I'd guess in his forties, and always dressed smartly in a brown sports jacket, casual slacks and shoes. He walked the same route as most fans after each match: down Cold Blow Lane, left onto Brocklehurst Street and then left onto Hatcham Park Road, onto Harts Lane and then left again towards New Cross Gate station. On most days he walked this walk with everyone else unnoticed. On days when scores elsewhere were of vital importance to a relegation or promotion battle, he was the most popular man in New Cross. This was because he carried with him a large radio. Not the small pocket transistor type that you could secrete in a pocket and listen to with headphones or press to your ear, but the kind that you'd find on kitchen or bathroom window sills that broadcast radio programmes around the house.

He would walk purposely along the road, cradling this large radio in his arm, with Radio Two's Sports Report programme blaring out. The walk to the station would almost always feature the first few match reports or summaries from the day's top matches but by the time he reached the platform at New Cross Gate, it would always be close to five o'clock, which meant one thing: the famous Sports Report music, the unmistakeable 'Out of the Blue' written by Hubert Bath.

This tune would alert other fans on the platform, meerkat-like, craning their necks to see where it was emanating from, because as all football fans know, this music means just one thing: final scores. As the equally recognisable velvet tones of James Alexander Gordon began the classified football results reading, a hush descended on the platform and a crowd gathered around Radio Man to hear the scores of the day. Then a weird thing happened: Radio Man got the hump. Cherishing your personal space is understandable. It's a common human trait almost as old as civilisation itself. But if you crave solitude, here's a bit of advice: don't stand on a busy train platform full of football fans desperate to know the football results, with a great big radio broadcasting the scores at high volume.

Once JAG was about three matches in, the charade would begin. With a loud and irritated sigh, Radio Man would turn on his heels and make steadily down the platform, followed of course by his new friends desperate not to miss the broadcast. This would now draw even more attention to him and attract new followers. Eventually, Radio Man would run out of platform, reaching that sloping bit that goes down to the tracks, so he'd turn 180 degrees and make his way back the other way again – with all of his fellow listeners in tow of course. By the time he had returned to his original position, others had witnessed the ritual and yet we'd only be half way through the Second Division results. So off he went again, towards the end of the platform, pursued now by even more eager hangers on. Once he returned for the second time, most of the key final scores had been announced and there was little interest in how Torquay or Halifax had fared. There was however some fun to be had. His disgruntlement at the sheer cheek of people wanting to share his public broadcast was not hidden. His sighs and head-shakes brought out the devil in many fans who were now following him on purpose, purely for the fun of it. By the time our train pulled into the station his pace had quickened and a giggling line of fans were tailing him up and down the platform, often letting out mocking fake cries of "Yes!" on hearing that Montrose had won 1-0 away to Dumbarton. As our train pulled away from the platform that day we had heard, thanks to Radio Man, all we needed to hear. Results elsewhere had gone our way, this was on, but we needed to beat Leeds.

Do you remember when there was an eclipse and the teachers at school would tell you not to look up at the sun? Almost every child, most of whom had no interest whatsoever in astronomy up until that point, would then make sure they did just that. I'm sure there's a fancy term for it. The awkward so-and-so effect, or something a little more technical perhaps. Anyway, it is this same science that applies to football fans – in particular Millwall supporters – when told not to attend a match.

Back in 1985, Millwall were due to play an away league match at Bournemouth just after the ill-fated FA Cup quarter final match at Luton where the infamous riot took place. Bournemouth decided to cancel on Police advice and the match was rearranged for later in the season. Away fans were asked not to attend but, with Millwall on the verge of promotion, that was never going to happen. Other measures were put in place to dissuade Lions fans from turning up. The kick off was brought forward to the rather ludicrous time of 6.30pm and away fans would be charged the extortionate admission price of £7.50 – with £5 refunded afterwards if there was no trouble. As with Radio Man, telling Millwall fans "no" was a red rag to a bull and almost certainly prompted many who had no intention of travelling to make an extra special effort that evening.

Perhaps learning their lesson, the club didn't go as far as asking Millwall fans to stay away from Leeds, but the local constabulary announced that it would be in their best interests not to bother as no trains would be available to get them home after the evening kick-off. If they thought that was enough to put them off supporting their team in arguably one of the biggest matches of its history they were sadly mistaken. As the match kicked off I found myself alone in the house. Dad had taken the week off work and he and Mum were visiting family in Kent, they wouldn't be home until after nine that evening. After battling the butterflies for most of the day, I had everything set up once kick-off time came round.

The living room television was set to its usual teletext latest score page. The second TV in the dining room was also on. This second set had been acquired second hand to allow me and Dad to get our teletext fix without disturbing Mum's evening viewing. By our family's standards it was a gesture of some decadence – a second telly? Whatever next? A Ferguson Videostar? My reason for having the latest scores on two televisions in different rooms was to test a theory that the latest scores were reported at different times on different sets. A sort of naivety meets grossly – exaggerated superstition and plain stupidity I guess, but I had the house to myself so why not try it out? Looking back now it makes no sense at all, but that's what the stress of following your team from afar can do to you.

Once kick-off time arrived I fidgeted from the arm chair in the front room to the kitchen, then out into the back garden for a quick breathe of fresh air, eventually finishing up sat on the stairs. All this in the name of killing some time before checking both sets' latest score and hoping we had taken the lead.

I didn't have to wait long. After what felt like an hour touring the house and garden, I walked into the front room at the very moment the screen flickered its change and reported that Tony Cascarino had given Millwall a 1-0 lead in the seventh minute. I leapt around the house from room to room shouting at the top of my voice and wishing I had someone to share the moment of elation with. As I calmed myself, I was reminded that in the remaining 80-odd minutes of football, a lot could happen.

I spent the rest of the first half caught up in my roaming ritual. God knows what the neighbours must have thought was going on. I took the opportunity to rest during the half time break, as exhausted as if I'd been playing at Elland Road myself.

The second half played out pretty much the same way, I returned to the front room after dong a few laps of the house once the 'HT' had disappeared from the latest score to indicate the game had resumed and, uncannily, as I entered the room again the screen flashed it's new report of: 'Leeds 0, Millwall 2 (Cascarino 7, Hurlock 49). I took off again around the house. Whenever I watch the film 'Home Alone 'at Christmas and the scene of Kevin running around the house having discovered he has it to himself plays out, I'm instantly reminded of how the 15-year-old me must have looked that evening. I was now in full-blown football fan neurosis. Estimating that there was approximately 40 minutes left allowing for the time it took teletext to report the goal and injury time, I started counting off the seconds and minutes in my head, promising myself not to look at either television until I had counted off 20 minutes. After the first count of 20 I edged slowly into the front room almost too scared to look at the screen. To my relief, it still reported that Millwall were 2-0 ahead, although I noticed from the clock on the wall that my time estimating skills left a lot to be desired, only ten minutes having elapsed since Hurlock's strike.

My next time-killing plan was to rearrange my bedroom. After what I thought was enough reorganising of CDs, records and cassette tapes to have taken us at least to the last five minutes I caught sight of my clock radio: just another ten minutes gone. After throwing myself on my bed and trying to calm myself with some slow breathing which only irritated me more, I heard the sound of the key in front door. I bound downstairs to find Mum and Dad returning home from their day out.

"Why are all the lights on?"

"Why are all the doors open?"

"Why have you got two televisions on and you're not watching either of them?"

"Have you been out in the gar – 'ere, the back door's unlocked – was that you? Are you tryin' to get us burgled?

Mum was firing off all the questions that bother parents when they've left you in the house on your own for a few hours, Dad meanwhile was on his way into the front room and immediately saw the TV, I followed him in.

"They're winning!" He exclaimed. I shot a look at the TV.

"No!" I shrieked. Dad looked puzzled.

The score was now 2-1. A Leeds penalty in the 71st minute meant that disaster was just the few seconds that it takes to score a goal away. A quick look at the clock showed me there was around ten minutes left. I couldn't bear the thought of going through that hellish last 600 seconds in the company of my parents and decided to make my exit. I figured a walk around the block would take up those final precious minutes. Of course, it wouldn't stop Leeds getting an equaliser – or worse, a winner too – but I'd rather spare myself any further anguish by just finding out when it was all over.

I flew out of the front door with my dad looking non-plussed and the sound of my mum ringing in my ears:

"You've left the bloody bathroom light on as well…"

I walked the route that my evening paper round took me. The same round that had funded much of my away travel that season. I prayed that it was going to prove an investment in witnessing the ultimate prize: promotion to the First Division. I made my way back up my path and realised that in my haste to leave I hadn't taken my key. I rang the doorbell and in seconds my dad appeared.

Dad was terrible at acting, and could never feign any emotion as part of a practical joke, so his huge grin as he stood in the warmly lit hallway told me everything I needed to know: it had finished Leeds 1, Millwall 2.

I was in a state of shock. We'd won. We'd actually won at Leeds. We were second in the table! After all those games, the hope, the despair, the seemingly endless and ultimately fruitless battle to gain one of those precious top two automatic promotion spots over the last seven months we had finally done it, with just five games left. It was in our hands. I looked at Dad.

"You bloody idiot, about 30 seconds after you shut the door the game finished." He chuckled.

I needed to toughen up my stress game, especially for the final few matches.

Three days later we were back at The Den. There was little doubt that this glut of home games – four out of the last five – was proving a huge advantage and even that point against Palace was starting to look like one gained as all around us major players in this crackpot farcical theatre production fluffed their lines.

Steve was conspicuous by his absence as we took our places, his dad Terry grinned a mischievous grin as he informed us he'd be coming along later. Meanwhile, one of our little terrace group of friends that had grown throughout the season was telling us about his trip to Leeds.

He said that he'd managed to get the train there early in the afternoon and found a large busy pub on the outskirts of the city. As he made his way to the bar he was eventually served by a nervous looking young man who had clearly been recruited to help with the sudden busy period. After ordering a pint of Fosters, the young host explained that he wouldn't be able to serve him. When our friend enquired why, he was told that were unable to serve away fans. It wasn't just his accent that gave him away but the fact that his blue Millwall home shirt was clearly visible under his open jacket. Having a quick look around, he was sure that he recognised a few faces as being Millwall supporters and wondered how they had managed to get served. Instinctively he threw both arms in the air and let out an almighty: "MMMMMMMMMMIIIIIIIIIIIIIIIIIIIII". The pub immediately erupted in full voice as every single drinker to a man joined the infamous chant.

Leaning across the bar so that he could be heard above the din, he looked the young barman in the eye and repeated his order: "Pint of Fosters, please".

He claimed to have mini-cabbed it to Doncaster station after the match in order to catch the last train home. We did wonder just how much of this tale was true, even though he produced a suitably crumpled match programme from his pocket to dispel any doubts – but that could easily have been obtained from our old friend Jimmy in the programme shop – but we let him have his moment of glory, either way it was a cracking story.

Plymouth, with nothing to play for, arrived at The Den as our stooges en-route to the big time. Dad was quick to pour cold water on our bravado however, telling us of the day back in 1966 that a very average Plymouth side visited The Den, which at the time was a fortress defending a record 59 league games unbeaten run. The expected rolling over of the west-country men to make it a nice round 60 never happened and the defeat was taken to heart, with the frustrations being taken out on the Plymouth coach afterwards.

The older heads around us nodded and hummed sagely at my dad's story, but there was another entirely different elephant in the room that afternoon. With just minutes to go before kick-off, Steve had arrived, and he wasn't alone. Steve had broken our solemn code: he'd brought his girlfriend to the match.

He introduced us to Nikki. She was a very pretty, petite blonde girl, clearly very shy and apprehensive of being in the midst of such a cauldron of male-dominated football tension.

I made a mental note to filter every outburst as to its suitability for female ears. I was the only one of course. What this actually meant was that I said absolutely nothing at all as the game started. My self-imposed muting only served to increase the tension.

Others of course were not as perturbed and continued to swear like pissed-up dockers with piles as Millwall started the latest chapter in a succession of 'most important games in our history' in less than convincing fashion.

Almost straight away, Plymouth took the lead.

"There are, told you, that'll be it now, they'll beat us just like they did down here when we were 59 unbeaten…" came the ridiculous comment from my dad. He always insisted 'that was it' if the other team took an early 1-0 lead, he was very rarely correct. His crazy observation angered me even more and I tried to find a way to take the heat out of the tension around us.

"It's all your fault, you're a bloody jinx, we were doing great until you came" I shouted at Nikki, jabbing an accusatory finger at her. It was of course meant in jest, but my brain clearly hadn't had time to adjust either my facial expression or tone sufficiently to make that clear. She looked petrified; believing every word I said was true. I was horrified. Steve reassured her I was only joking but I'm not sure he was convinced himself and didn't seem very happy with me; either that or the fact that he was regretting breaking our 'no birds at the match' rule. It was created for a reason Steve.

Thankfully the tension was eased minutes later when we were awarded a penalty, which Kevin O'Callaghan coolly rammed home. Remember what I said about that man and his penalties? You haven't seen anything yet…

Seconds later Cascarino gave us the lead with a stupendous overhead kick and two minutes after that Sheringham made it three. It was just after ten past three and we'd seen four goals, with the hope now of a record-breaking final tally. It didn't come, in fact Plymouth scored again in the 25th minute but by that point they had given up the ghost, I had been able to apologise several times over to Nikki and the game was over as a contest by half time. We were top. Top of the league. Talk about timing. We were playing it like a racehorse staying up with the leaders for the majority of the race and then hitting the front in the final furlongs.

Plymouth's chief tormentor had been our winger Jimmy Carter. He was a slight, frail-looking player who had arrived the previous season on a free transfer from QPR. He showed encouraging occasional glimpses of pace and trickery in his first few games but was strangely absent at the start of this season after suffering the ignominy of being subbed on, then off again during a League Cup second leg game against Orient at The Den back in August.

Only later in the season when he regained his place and started to show the sparkling form, blistering pace and incisory crossing that helped to catapult us up the table did we discover the real reason surrounding his hiatus: bananas.

Apparently, keen to bulk up his light frame, believing it would help his game, he'd been recommended 'the banana diet' and he promptly began to function purely on bunch after bunch of the starchy yellow delicacy. This harks back to an era where players where left to their own devices nutritionally. There were no strict diet plans for Docherty's troops - they were professionals and it was assumed they knew how to live in order to deliver the goods come 3pm on Saturday.

It was only when Docherty and his assistant Frank McLintock started to notice a sudden downturn in Carter's main asset – his speed – that they decide to investigate. Docherty discovered Carter had brought with him to training a large leather holdall, not full of kit, but brimming with great yellow fists of Fyffes' finest.

When Carter explained his build-up diet plan the penny immediately dropped as to why his lightning pace had deserted him. While he was bulking up, he was of course slowing down. Not to mention the fact that he must have been constipated beyond belief too, being stuffed with more starch than a sergeant major's shirt collar.

Freed of his tropical handicap, Carter in full flow was a joy to behold. His legs were a zig-zagging blur and his acceleration through the gears as he bamboozled flat-footed opposition defenders raised the fans' excitement another octave.

Frustratingly, it would be another ten days before Millwall would be able to try and cement their newly-found top dog status. It would be ten days of apprehension that, now they were at the top of the pile, did they have the mental strength not to get knocked off – or had they peaked just a little too soon?

In truth, the rest was probably invaluable for the team. Whilst three of their promotion rivals took part in the farcical Centenary tournament at Wembley, Millwall were relaxing and preparing for their midweek trip to Bournemouth.

Just like in 1985, a midweek trip to the idyllic south coast town was an opportunity for Millwall to put themselves on the brink of promotion. Thankfully, unlike 1985, there were no such restrictions in place to prevent the fans from attending.

I travelled on the official away supporters' club coach with Lloyd. It was one of those warm spring evenings that put you in the mood for summer and gives you that indescribable warm glow that makes you feel like "everything's going to work out OK". Football doesn't subscribe to that way of thinking of course. In fact it often takes great pride in pulling the rug from under you as soon as you venture into any such feelings of liberation. As always, I was ready for us to have glory cruelly snatched from our hands, although I knew that with every passing game, its security was almost assured. A win at Bournemouth and another in the next home game against Stoke could leave us just needing a win at Hull. It was almost too fantastic to even consider, for fear of experiencing even the merest hint of the feeling of being a First Division team in less than two weeks.

Millwall dominated the opening minutes of the match in an atmosphere that was as good as that of any home game. Away from home you're making a statement as a fan. The impetus is on you to let the home fans you're there. It's OK for them to wait until the action on the pitch stirs them into action. It's important to get into character the second you disembark the coach or train, throughout the Police escort to the ground and as soon as you emerge the other side of the turnstiles.

After just ten minutes of intense Millwall pressure, the referee pointed to the spot and awarded Millwall another penalty – our second in two games. This was unheard of. You could go seasons at a time and not see your team given a spot kick. This was our third in total and with a penalty taker like Kevin O'Callaghan, it was as good as a goal.

Just over ten minutes later a looping Terry Hurlock half volley nestled beneath the cross bar and into the roof of the Bournemouth net to make it 2-0. The away end behind the goal bounced in a joyous rhythm like a swelling ocean ebbing and flowing, the foam of arms and fists spilling between the bars of the perimeter fence as the players celebrated in front of them.

Just to keep our minds on the task at hand, Tony Pulis (yes, that one) pulled a goal back for Bournemouth soon after and we went into the half time break breathless, elated, but mindful there was still a little way to go.

Single goal leads are bad for the heart, but it was something we were growing accustomed to dealing with. Until now, with the exception of that last gasp Palace equaliser, we had managed to hold on with little incident in our various single goal victories against Villa, Leeds and Plymouth. Like I said, until now…

The whistling to encourage the referee to blow for full time was starting to trigger a panic reaction in me. I instantly associated it with everything that was bad about watching football: last minute heartache. The sound of the referee's whistle – and even the cheers that greeted it from the home fans - was barely audible above the shrill din emanating from our terrace, but it soon became apparent what had happened. The ref hadn't blown for full time, he'd given Bournemouth a penalty, in the last minute.

The wait for the spot kick to be taken was agony. In our favour, the Bournemouth penalty taker would have to face the three thousand or so Millwall fans who would obviously do whatever it took to distract him. Watching in sickening anticipation, we stared at the ball, stationery on the spot, and willed it to be missed while others waved their arms wildly and leapt up and down. Being towards the back of the packed terrace, all we saw was the run up, the strike, and the ball disappear from its whitewashed indent. The next sight that greeted us was of Millwall goalkeeper Brian Horne on his feet, to the left of his goal, ball safely clutched in right arm, left fist held aloft in celebration. Seconds later it was all over.

Back at The Den, the match had been relayed on a giant screen for fans who couldn't get tickets as supply once again far outstripped demand, with commentary provided by the legendary Kenneth Wolstenholme, whose famous "They think it's all over, it is now" line which narrated England's World Cup win at Wembley in 1966 had been immortalised. For Millwall, it wasn't quite all over just yet though, and that late penalty was a cautionary tale of how quickly it could all go wrong.

As goalkeepers go, Brian Horne was an unlikely looking candidate. They were often at least six feet in height, preferably freakishly taller than that, and yet in my brief time following Millwall, none of our 'keepers had been particularly tall or possessed the spade-like hands of Pat Jennings. At 5' 9" or so, 'Horney' often looked lost between the posts, and yet was one of the most acrobatic shot stoppers I've ever seen. When he broke in to the side as a 19-year-old, a prospect of the club's youth team, fans cut him plenty of slack. He didn't need it. Playing in a struggling team during John Docherty's first season, he quickly made the number one shirt his own, leaving previous first choice Paul Sansome – who had rarely put a foot wrong and was popular with the fans – out in the cold. Horne was another local boy, someone who followed the club as a kid from the terraces, and now, still six months short of his 21st birthday, was on the verge of achieving what no other player had done in Millwall's 103 year history. Horne was the spring-heeled dynamo between the sticks whose incongruous stature proved that, just like his team, it wasn't the size of the dog in the fight, but the size of fight in the dog.

You can't really ask for much more from your team than to be two points clear at the top of the league with three matches left to play, especially when two of those games are in front of your own supporters. However, at Millwall there is a precarious tipping point on such occasions. The white-hot big match atmosphere at The Den can quickly turn to frustrated silence if an early goal doesn't settle those thinly disguised nerves. The promotion places had settled since the turn of the year with Aston Villa leading the way and Bradford, Palace, Middlesbrough and Blackburn jostling with Millwall for the next five places. Leeds had their noses pressed firmly against the glass in the forlorn hope of a late invite to the play-offs, but that had been ended by their home defeat to Millwall – which made The Lions' result all the more impressive. Villa and Blackburn had wobbled at the crucial time when it looked as though both would secure the top two positions in April, leaving the rest to fight over the scraps, and allowing Millwall's perfectly timed run to nudge them into pole position.

The maths was simple: three games left, win them all, win promotion. There were a few flies in the ointment however. Millwall didn't really do long winning runs, they were currently on one of the best in recent years as it was – five on the bounce since that Palace draw – could they really make it eight straight victories, or had they hit the front just that little bit too early? Stoke were perfectly set to be party poopers – they had nothing to play for so would be relaxed but certainly not in any mood to throw the game with players possibly looking to secure a new contract for the following season. They had been the team to stop Blackburn in their tracks – ending their record-breaking 23-game unbeaten streak. Millwall's goal difference was not favourable either, being inferior by several goals to the teams breathing down their necks and waiting for them to slip up. Even beating Stoke would leave them needing a win away to Hull – who despite slipping out of the promotion frame themselves, had lost just three times at their Boothferry Park ground that season, then Blackburn would be the final visitors to The Den. First Division promotion heartache at The Den on the last day of the season in the company of visitors from Lancashire was just far too familiar a scenario for those fans still scarred by the events of 1972 when Millwall finished in third place just two seasons before two promotion places were increased to three – could they conceivably finish third this time around – two seasons after those automatic prizes had been reduced back down to two again?

In Millwall's favour was the fact that Villa weren't playing, and one of their remaining two games was against rivals Bradford. Another six-pointer was happening as Millwall kicked off against Stoke with Blackburn visiting Palace. As the process of reducing the top division from 22 to 20 clubs was half complete, a 23 team Second Division meant that each weekend one team sat it out, just another bizarre fixture twist to sit alongside the weekend break for the Wembley centenary party debacle. So the permutations were sending Millwall fans into a frenzy as the tense opening minutes unfolded. Confusion over who had played how many and which teams were facing each other and the impact these variables had on their potential points tallies was distraction that only served to fuel the growing frustration as Millwall tried to chip away at a stubborn Stoke defence. Half time arrived with no breakthrough and news that Bradford were leading meant they were now tied on points with Millwall and Middlesbrough also led, putting them within two points of The Lions. Blackburn trailed at Palace which had almost become a play-off for the play-offs, although there would be one last twist in that particular tale.

The second half started brightly, with Millwall looking more purposeful and Stoke slightly less interested in spoiling the occasion. Five minutes in, right back Keith Stevens lofted a speculative diagonal ball from just inside the Stoke half. It hung in the air for an age before dropping dangerously among a ruck of players. First to it was a Stoke defender but, under pressure from O'Callaghan, he was only able to head it across the face of his goal and into the path of Sheringham who coolly volleyed into the bottom right corner of the net from eight yards out. The cheer that greeted it was understandably punctuated with relief but now the shackles were off and 12 minutes later Millwall were awarded a third penalty in three games which O'Callaghan slotted home to seal the match.

With a five point cushion over third place and just six points to play for, Millwall were almost there. Promotion to the First Division for the first time was finally within their grasp, only the long journey to Hull stood between them and being able to actually touch it.

12
THE ROAD TO HULL

My impatience to commit to being at Hull meant that instead of the usual official away travel route, I was going courtesy of a pub-organised coach trip which had been advertised in the local paper a few weeks before Millwall put their tickets on sale. My cousin Glen had agreed to go with me. Ten years my senior, Glen was a self-confessed football anorak. Whilst he had followed Palace through his teens in the seventies, this was mainly fueled by his curiosity to visit as many grounds as possible – a mission which was greatly helped by Palace's climb from Third Division to First and an appearance in an FA Cup semi-final. He and his dad Stan also enjoyed taking in games at local non-league Tooting and Mitcham and had also followed Wimbledon's rise from non-league to top flight football. In fact, in the previous decade, Glen had managed to watch two teams do what Millwall had waited over ten times as long to experience – win promotion to the top flight. He was keen to watch a bit of history being made. So at 7:30 on a chilly May Bank Holiday Monday morning we made our way through the quiet south London streets in Stan's old white Escort for the first leg of the road to Hull.

A face appeared at the window of the Bricklayers Arms pub. A lady in her fifties mouthed the question "Millwall?" and as we nodded, the sound of metal bolts being released and the heavy black wooden door being pushed open split the quiet morning air along with the unmistakable sound of voices chatting and glasses clinking.

The lady took my name and firmly drew a line through it on a sheet of paper weighted down with an empty pint glass on a small table to the right of the door.

"Drink?" she offered as she made for the bar.

We politely declined; all around us fans were sat at tables and it looked as though the party had started early – or was continuing late from the previous night. Pint glasses in various stages of emptiness filled the tables. The subdued buzz of a pub full of expectant and nervous football fans at 8am turned into eager cheers as the coach appeared outside.

The journey was slow and uneventful. All of the fixtures and fittings remained intact and the effects of the early morning/late night session took its toll with most of the journey being made in sleepy silence.

As we made our way across the Humber Bridge and into Hull the coach exploded into life with songs and chants to announce our arrival. Passers-by gawped at us as the freak show arrived in town. With more than two hours to go before kick-off, these were couples and families popping out to make the most of the Bank Holiday sunshine. The town itself was a welcome change from the other away trips. Rather than dark gloomy side streets with rows and rows of terraced houses bearing down on us, Hull was bright wide tree-lined roads, with pleasant grass verges trimming well-kept homes with good sized front gardens.

Our coach came to a stop in the car park of a large supermarket which had been built into one end of the ground. A legacy of boom and bust times, Hull had been a big team on the up in the sixties with a large ground to match their own top flight ambitions but the town suffered more than most during the lean times of the seventies and eighties – and its team went into alarming decline too, almost going out of business on several occasions and part of one end of the ground was sold to developers turning the large terrace behind the goal into a narrow enclosure. Their recovery began alongside Millwall's when they gained promotion with The Lions from the

Third Division in 1985 but the ground, like Millwall's Den was a crumbling relic and stark reminder of the hard times both clubs were desperate to leave behind.

We entered the ground to find we had been given a large part of the wing terrace and the small strip of terracing behind the goal at the supermarket end. We also had seating in the opposite wing stand which was a compact little structure not unlike our own main stand at The Den. As we took a place half way up the at corner of the two terraces we could see other coaches carefully edging their way in and out of the car park and the trickle of Millwall fans appearing from the turnstile doors soon turned into a steady flow. By 2pm both terraces were filling out and the noise levels were raised another notch as the football special train arrived at the Boothferry Halt station and emptied another couple of hundred fans into the stadium. As the minutes ticked by painfully slowly, the clear blue spring sky gradually turned white then grey and as heavy dark clouds surrounded us a flash of lightning and rumble of thunder ushered in a torrential downpour that sent fans scurrying for cover. It passed as quickly as it arrived, but the brief storm only added a sense of drama to the occasion. The noise noticeably faded back to a palpably nervous buzz, and erupted once again as the teams emerged from the tunnel. This was it, 103 years in the making, 90 minutes that would go down in the club's history as the day they finally made it – or the day they once again came so close – only to fall at the final hurdle.

In some ways I envied Glen. As a neutral he was able to relax and enjoy the occasion and found my clearly visible nerves quite amusing as I spent most of my time hopping anxiously from one foot to the next, like a little kid desperate for a piss but unable to go. Then again, for all the stress he was being spared, he would have none of the joy that we were investing so heavily in if the result went our way. Looking back, I think a big part of the pressure I was feeling was not only for my own desperate need to see us succeed, but I now felt like I was on a season-long mission to bring this previously unachieved feat to fruition not just personally – but for my dad. That morning, I had not only set off to Hull in order to watch my team clinch the points required to secure promotion, but I'd become like some medieval crusader setting off to war in a distant land with the intention of returning home victorious with the spoils for his king.

We just needed an early goal.

After looking at my watch yet again and noticing it was only ten past three, it also occurred to me that I had barely watched the football being played out in front of me. I found it impossible not to panic when Hull even touched the ball for fear of an early home goal and chose instead to turn away and watch the different emotions being displayed in the crowd. Some, like me, were looking everywhere but at the pitch; others looked fixed to the action, almost hypnotised by it, heading every ball, and thrusting their bodies into every tackle as they were made. Nails were being bitten, jokes offered to try and quell the nerves. Elsewhere many were in more confident mood, treating the day like a coronation. Until we at least had that vital goal I simply couldn't even contemplate that. My biggest fear was of a huge capitulation, being 3-0 down at half time and hearing other scores all going against us, watching it all fall apart after being seemingly so perfectly choreographed for the past few weeks.

As I craned my neck to get a good view of a Millwall throw-in deep in the Hull half, which was difficult enough in the large swaying crowd but made harder by the fact they were attacking the opposite end, the huge looping ball which was a Keith Stevens speciality aimed at the Hull penalty area disappeared for a split second and then as it came down and was headed on into the six yard box it was pinged goalwards by Sheringham. The goalkeeper got a hand to it but it looked to be in from our distant vantage point. We jumped and then saw the ball suddenly back in play. The sound of the referee's whistle punctuated our shouts, initially believing the ball had been illegally scooped out from behind the line by a Hull defender, some started to celebrate believing the goal had been given but it soon became apparent as the ref took his position twelve yards from the goal:

Penalty to Millwall.

By the time the news had sunk in to every single away fan, Kevin O'Callaghan was making his familiar run up. It was a routine we had now become familiar with, for the fourth consecutive match, the penalty was ruthlessly converted and our nerves – both on and off the pitch – dissolved.

For the rest of the first half Millwall assaulted the Hull goal in an attempt to make the game safe before the break. Minutes later a Sheringham header from a deep O'Callaghan cross rattled back off the post and from the resulting corner Cascarino's point-blank effort from inside the six yard box was somehow scrambled clear.

The centre circle had become a mud bath which was so typical of the pitches of the era and Terry Hurlock made it his own territory with trademark crunching tackles winning every ball that entered it. It was hard to believe we had reached half time with just that tenth minute penalty to our advantage. Hull were gamely competing but wilting under the bombardment and the realisation that this was Millwall's day began to dawn on players and fans alike as the second half started at a less furious tempo.

As the game moved into its final quarter the second goal that we craved so desperately to relieve that final bit of tension and allow us to fully enjoy the occasion just wouldn't come. A Cascarino header took a wicked deflection and Hull 'keeper Tony Norman was stranded as the ball looped over his head but it continued its trajectory just inches over the bar and into the away fans behind the goal. Then Millwall robbed Hull of possession in their own half and a deft ball forward by Hurlock fell beautifully for Cascarino whose acrobatic volley looked to be arrowing goalwards – only for Norman to pull off a stunning stop. The grey gave way to bright sunshine again as my watch showed 88 minutes had been played, Hull sensed a later spoiler and pushed forward, Millwall looked leg-weary having used every drop of energy ploughing through the mud in search of a killer goal. I couldn't take it anymore.

I pushed my way through the crowds and headed for the toilet block at the back of the narrow terrace behind the goal with the plan to kill the last few minutes in a stinking away end urinal. As I entered I was amazed to see dozens of fans had the same idea. They were smoking and pacing up and down like expectant fathers, tapping their watches and dashing to the entrance of the ramshackle brick building every time they heard an encouraging cheer from their fellow fans. After what felt like an age I checked my watch again, eight minutes to five.

Back in 1988 we had no such luxury of announcements of how much time would be added on, the length of this torture was completely unknown, but by my reckoning we had played 48 minutes in the second half. I started to make my way back to Glen on the terrace just as Sheringham cut inside the Hull left and made for goal, his shot from just outside the penalty area swerved wildly wide and hit the fencing just in front of me. Hull took the goal kick quickly and returned the ball to Norman's hands for one last booming clearance to jangle our nerves. The ball pinged around the centre circle as I took my place next to Glen once more who was laughing again at my frantic disposition and prolonged toilet break. I turned to face the pitch, the referee held his right arm aloft and blew his whistle. It was over.

The first thing that hits you, after you celebrate the end of such a game in the same way you'd celebrate a goal is: what do we do now? The Millwall fans who had chosen to sit in the stand had been able to run on to the pitch and players were quickly mobbed and relieved of shirts, but they seemed to have a similar dilemma to me and were wandering quite aimlessly around the pitch at first. Most of us were confined to the terraces, the same rotating spikes that adorned the top of The Den perimeter fences prevented a mass pitch celebration. Once the players had managed to organise themselves into some semblance of a lap of honour to salute the fans on the terraces, news came through that Bradford had lost at Aston Villa. Millwall were champions.

It was one of those times in your life that you wanted to go on forever. Then it occurred to you that there was even better to come. I don't think I've ever looked forward to a five hour coach journey as much as the one that awaited us that evening. I was looking forward to relaxing on the coach, closing my eyes and reliving every shot, goal, celebration, heartache; every peak and trough of that incredible season over and over in my head. I wanted to speak to my dad. I'd begged him to come, but he flatly refused. His official reason was that he had to be at work at six on the Tuesday morning and he didn't want a late night but I knew that was a very poor cover story for the real reason: that he couldn't bear to see his beloved Millwall fail again.

The jubilant players finally made their way down the tunnel to continue their party in the more private confines of the dressing room. The songs continued on the terraces but fatigue was kicking in. Fans were visibly exhausted; faces were red with exuberance, voices already cracking from the non-stop shouting and singing. I saw some older fans visibly emotional, wiping a tear, shaking their heads in disbelief. Again I wanted to speak to my dad, remembering his words about never living to see The Lions in the top flight, my only hope was to call from a payphone during a services stop-off on the way home.

As we slowly exited the ground into the car park and looked for our coach, fans were dancing on top of a minibus and dousing themselves in beer from cans one can only assume had been stashed in their vehicles ready to toast success or drown their sorrows.

We took our seats and our coach slowly made its way onto the main road. The stereo was tuned to Radio Two where it was soon clear we were the lead news story. Alan Green was painting a picture of the day for listeners in his unmistakable northern Irish tones. Voices such as Green's and the equally distinctive ones of Peter Jones and Jimmy Armfield were usually reserved for football royalty, live Radio Two broadcasts of top matches in Division One, the latter stages of the FA Cup or European competitions. Now little old Millwall were worthy of the same attention that Arsenal, Tottenham, Everton, Liverpool and Manchester United enjoyed week in week out and next season we'd find ourselves officially in their company.

To add to the surreal feeling of it all, passers-by, many in Hull colours, waved, clapped and gave us thumbs-up signals as we provided the locals with another chorus of "No-one Likes Us". For a few minutes, it felt like everyone did. The headline that screamed out of a tabloid's typically hysterical match report from our FA Cup match at Arsenal of "Please God don't let Millwall win promotion" felt a million miles away now. So too the empty sick feeling in my stomach when that ball pinged down off Jim Cannon's hand and he toed it over the line to rob us of a vital win over Palace and the merciless mickey taking I had to endure from Cheryl's mum and dad that evening. As we left Hull behind us, I spent a few moments thinking about all the moments during that season where all had seemed lost, but how every single one had been worth it, just to say: "I was there".

As our party clambered off the coach for a services stop and made for the toilets or to grab some much-needed refreshment I had only one thing on my mind: call Dad. I found a phone box and within seconds I could hear his excited voice at the other end of the line.

"Dad!" I shouted. As I did, a fellow fan passing the booth heard me and banged on the window and laughing, playfully mocked: "Dad, dad, we've won the league.."

He was expecting my call.

"You should've come Dad, it was amazing, I told you we'd do it"

That was a lie of course. My aborted attempt at some father and son bonding a couple of months earlier following the revelations of my conception had been temporarily wiped from my mind. Somewhere in there we shared that cosy moment where I reassured him this was the year he'd finally see his team make up for the heartache of 1972. It's just now I felt it was more than just the football that had disappointed him back then. Hopefully our shared passion for Millwall had justified my existence now? I felt as though I had travelled to Hull to bring home something that he lost all those years before and with it gain his approval.

We spoke briefly and I said I'd see him later, he said he'd be in bed long before I arrived home. I knew he wouldn't be.

Glen then called his dad to let him know roughly what time we were due to arrive back. The Bank Holiday traffic meant his estimate was about an hour out, but Stan was about as easy-going a man as you're ever likely to meet and he was sat waiting patiently for us when the coach pulled in just after 11pm.

I turned my key in the door and closed it behind me as quietly as possible; as soon as I did I heard the sound of feet on the stairs. Dad came bounding down in his striped pyjamas and grabbed me with a huge smile on his face and we danced mad circles up and down the hallway singing different incoherent bits of different Millwall songs. Then I heard Mum's voice as she appeared at the top of the stairs:

"Stupid bleeder, wouldn't go to sleep until you came in, like a bloody kid…"

In exactly three weeks I would be officially leaving school, on my 16th birthday, and I fully intended to make the most of every single day, to make up for the previous four and half years of torment. Since September 1983 I had been ridiculed, first for actually going to football (as hard as it is to believe now, following a football team back in the early eighties was far from the fashionable pastime it is today) and then, as it became more acceptable, for the team I followed, being one of only two Millwall supporters in a school full of Palace fans. I was able to enjoy the brief thrill of us beating Palace in an FA Cup replay in 1985 but apart from that we'd been the poor relations. A couple of dead rubber late season wins over them at The Den didn't make up for defeats at Selhurst Park in the early weeks of the 1985/86 and 86/87 seasons, especially after we had taken the lead in both games.

Even more galling was the fact that the Palace winner in the latter fixture was scored by Anton Otulakowski – my favourite Millwall star of George

Graham's 1985 promotion-winning team. Things couldn't have possibly ended any better than Millwall finishing top of the pile just weeks before I left school could they? Well actually…

After beating Blackburn, Palace had lost their latest match at Leeds 1-0 while we were winning at Hull, an event not lost on us as our coach passed some of their fans on the M1 returning home. Suffice to say we didn't receive the same congratulations that Hull fans had afforded us, probably because every car we passed that displayed their red, white and blue colours in received dogs' abuse. For one particular stretch of the motorway, when Palace cars seemed to be everywhere, I caught the eye of the driver of one vehicle with scarves laid neatly on the back shelf. I gave them my sickliest gloating smile and the full range of offensive hand signals that I knew, finished off with an exaggerated wave as we gradually passed them. The driver of the vehicle glanced up and our eyes met, her initial look of disdain turned to disgust when she realised she knew me. It was Maureen, a work friend of my mum's who lived around the corner from us and went to every Palace game home and away. What were the chances?

Blackburn's draw in that penultimate game set up a final day of high drama as two teams had a chance of claiming that final play-off place. Aston Villa, Middlesbrough and Bradford would battle it out for second place, while Palace needed to beat Manchester City at home and hope that Blackburn lost their match: at Millwall.

So far from bristling at my celebration on my return to school – a favourite of which was to produce my Millwall-crested playing cards from my inside jacket pocket at the start of our regular break-time card games and announce that we were playing with "the First Division deck", the Palace contingent of my school were at their weaseley best.

They honestly expected me to swallow their feigned best wishes, and empty platitudes about how pleased they were for Millwall, all in the hope that we'd "do them a favour" and beat Blackburn the following Saturday to allow them their chance of joining us in Division One via the play-offs.

What was also noticeable was how the large bunch of so-called Palace fans who had never set foot inside a football stadium in their lives but were the most vocal after the two games between the teams that were suddenly uninterested in anything football-related.

"Aw, I'm really pleased, it's good for London football innit? Obviously Millwall would rather Palace were I the play-offs than Blackburn eh?" was the common theme.

"I hope we get thrashed" was my stock response.

The local television's sports roundup broadcasts were dominated by the weekend's final league fixtures. Palace fans watching must have been doubly sick to their stomachs hearing about the planned 'knees up' at The Den (the stock media description of every joyous occurrence at Millwall it seemed) and the fact that their own fate lie very much in the hands of their local foes who had already been crowned champions. Palace manager Steve Coppell was interviewed and asked the obvious question about needing Millwall to do his side the favour of winning an eighth consecutive league game that they really didn't need to do. I've never wanted Millwall to lose any match. But I had to admit, Blackburn at home on May 7th 1988 was the least I'd ever wanted us to win.

My teenage football fantasy came true on that perfect Saturday. Millwall home match days were magical – even during the hardest of times at The Den. I loved the routine: waking to the smell of breakfast cooking downstairs; soaking in the bath while listening to the radio and then watching Saint and Greavsie on the TV with a cup of tea in my Millwall mug and a spot of lunch before heading off with Dad to catch the train from Norwood Junction to New Cross Gate. It did occur to me at times that I was perhaps 15 going on 50, but I brushed this off. I was happy. A bit odd at times perhaps, but as happy as the proverbial pig in shit with my simple life: Millwall and music.

South Norwood was already starting to buzz with Palace fans on their way to their big play-off show-down. I felt the nervousness of the dozen or so stood outside the Cherry Trees pub as we walked into the station and grinned as they noticed my Millwall shirt. How they must have wished they were in our shoes.

We bought our tickets and took the underpass to platform three. We sat in the same wooden bench booth that we had done for the previous eight years that we had made that same journey. It was a routine repeated to monotonous efficiency, without a second thought, just as most pilgrimages are.

The train once again took us through Anerley, Penge West and Sydenham. I thought about how many times I must have gazed out of the window as we passed those stations over the years and wondered if our loyalty would ever be rewarded. As we moved on through Forest Hill, Honor Oak Park and Brockley I remembered the excitement of those journeys as we neared our destination during my first promotion season three years before, thinking nothing could beat that feeling. All that I'd experienced over the previous nine months had done just that and it would stay with me forever.

As our train emerged from the tunnel and slowed on the approach to New Cross Gate, I realised that whatever we achieved in the future no simple train journey to a football match would ever be this good again.

On New Year's Eve I had dreamt of a day at The Den in May. Of shirt-sleeved fans packed into the Cold Blow Lane and Halfway Line terraces, bathed in sunshine, waving flags and singing as the team paraded the Second Division champions' trophy around the touchline with the strains of Queen's We Are The Champions filling the air. Back then I had shaken that image from my head as a ridiculous piece of childish dreaming, one which I would look back on with embarrassment when the grim reality of mid-table obscurity was duly delivered in five months' time. If I'm perfectly honest, there was still a tinge of shame in recalling that moment, because it was a cringe-worthy departure of self-indulgence that a fifteen-year-old should have long since grown out of. But that's what football does to you.

It gets you dreaming of days like that just as a small child dreams of Christmas morning. It compels grown men to dance together, unashamedly hugging other men they have never met before on a crumbling terrace in the pouring rain in Sheffield to celebrate a last minute goal. It makes you put a simple football club before everything else in your life.

As the sun shone and the flags waved and the Championship trophy shone and Freddie Mercury sang, I afforded myself a little self-congratulatory chuckle. This was exactly as I had planned it. Spooky eh?

The match had long since sold out. The only disappointment was that the stadium's capacity had been reduced to just 15,000 thanks to safety measures and the restriction of the Ilderton Road terrace behind the goal being made 'Members Only'. Quite righty, Millwall fans had objected to such sanctions, dictated by the Football Association which the club reluctantly agreed to in order to avoid further punishment. As a result, those fans who preferred to watch from that terrace chose alternative areas to stand leaving it half empty for most games. The club said they could have sold the tickets three times over, of which there was little doubt. Thankfully our tickets were safe. I had persuaded Dad to invest in a season ticket the previous summer, something he was reluctant to do because of the initial expense. I'd saved and bought one for the previous three seasons, in my mind it was the sort of commitment that came as standard with following your team. Stories of fans who had been Den regulars for decades missing out on the biggest day in the club's history were doing the rounds in the build-up the week before and the resentment that surfaced over the coming season as home attendances rose from 4,000 to 16,000 was already starting to manifest itself.

There was a certain amount of surprise that the club decided to perform the formalities before the game, but it was certainly the right decision. It added to the carnival atmosphere and allowed every single member of that season's squad to get their fully deserved adulation.

They say you never appreciate the good times until you look back on them.

It was something that preyed on my mind often as a teenager and I started to feel the years pass gradually quicker. I probably wasted a fair amount of this valuable time thinking a little bit too much. Troubled by the saying: "The best years of your life are at school" throughout that final term, I asked my English teacher Mr Fullman if it was true. With a weary look, he leant towards me and whispered in my ear: "It's a load of bollocks". He was of course completely wrong, but I am forever grateful for him sparing me the anguish that my life was hurtling towards the end of its happy days at just fifteen.

That day I was only too aware of the preciousness of the moment and savoured every single second of it. There was almost a wave of disappointment as the trophy presentation paraphernalia was packed away and it became evident that there was a rather important football match still to be played.

By half time we were trailing by two goals. Millwall had been virtual spectators in a match that Blackburn had dominated in a thoroughly professional manner from the kick off – just as you'd expect them to. The disappointment that we wouldn't be finishing the season with another win and let history show a final league table of utter Millwall dominance by winning the division by a seven point margin soon dissipated at the half time break when we thought of how our capitulation would be being received over at Selhurst Park.

A Sheringham goal five minutes into the second half only served to prod Blackburn back to into action and they struck back three minutes afterwards to kill the game stone dead. The Millwall players had clearly spent the week celebrating and were feeling the effects of the biggest party the club had ever staged, and no-one could blame them. Another Blackburn goal five minutes from time drew some ironic boos from certain sections but now a joint celebration was starting up as we prepared to celebrate promotion one last time at the final whistle – and also our hand in Palace's ultimate misery.

Once again, as at Hull five days before, I didn't want the day to end. I wanted to press pause on that precise moment, because I knew, without any doubt, whatever the First Division brought us, this day, this moment, could never, ever be beaten.

Looking back, do I regret not being just a year or two older so that I could've celebrated 'properly' with the other fans, drinking into the small hours and actually enjoying the stinking hangover because it had been well and truly earned? Not a bit. My evening was spent going over all the various highs and lows of that season with Dad and enjoying one of those rare but enjoyable occasions when we chatted away to each other like best mates.

I've mentioned certain players from that historic season, and it's only fair to provide the full roll of honour for every single one that contributed to that fantastic achievement. These players were part of the dream becoming reality – even the ones who only played a single league game or made the briefest of cameo appearances, so here they are, in alphabetical order: Steve Anthrobus, Les Briley, David Byrne, Jimmy Carter Tony Cascarino, Nicky Coleman, Robbie Cooke, Brian Horne, Terry Hurlock, George Lawrence, Alan McLeary, Dave Mehmet, Darren Morgan, Kevin O'Callaghan, Danis Salman, Paul Sansome, Teddy Sheringham, Sean Sparham, Keith Stevens, David Thompson, Alan Walker and Steve Wood.

Congratulations gentlemen, you will forever be able to say: "I was there" and you helped make tens of thousands of humble little south London football fantasies come true.

The next day we had arranged to meet Steve and his dad in the local pub for a couple of lunchtime pints to once again relive the whole thing – and reassure ourselves that it had really happened. It was something we'd started doing on a few occasions that season, and the Sunday staff at The Portmanor Arms didn't seem to mind an obviously under-age drinker sat slowly supping a pint of Fosters while his companions knocked them back much quicker - and bought every round.

As I was grabbing a bite to eat before we set off, the radio was on in the kitchen – as it seemed to be on a permanent basis in my childhood days. It was the Radio One Dave Lee Travis show, snooker and darts on the radio and all that sort of thing, just background noise really. I was just about to the leave the room when I heard him make an announcement that the Witney Houston concert scheduled for that evening at Wembley had been cancelled. I chuckled because Rob and Tony, two Palace-supporting friends of mine from school, had tickets for it. Yep, that's right, Whitney Houston, I could never get my head around it either. I was going to wait until I was back in school the next day to really give it to the Palace lot, but I couldn't resist starting early so picked up the phone and called Rob.

To my surprise Rob and Tony were completely oblivious to the news. After taking a good few minutes abuse from Rob – with a sizeable background mouthful from Tony who was at his house ready to set off for Wembley – I explained that the radio had just announced the gig was off. He didn't believe me. Choking back the laughter, I tried to explain the announcement that I'd just heard but they still weren't convinced. I did also try to apologise for the fact that my team had clearly been so pissed from celebrating winning the league a full week early that they were in no fit state to help out their dear rivals from down the road, but they weren't swallowing that either. To be fair, that bit probably made the Whitney story a more likely candidate for a wind-up than when I'd first broke the news. There was of course no Internet to refer to and a quick scan of Teletext and the radio bulletins also drew a blank. I left them with my advice not to make the long tiresome journey down the Jubilee Line and set off for the pub with Dad.

At about eight thirty that evening the phone rang. It was Rob, and once again he was ranting. Apparently, not believing me, he and Tony did indeed travel to Wembley for the concert, only to see a sign when they got off the tube that the concert had been cancelled. Then, thanks to a combination of Sunday train times and engineering works, it was hours before they made it back home. Four to be precise, he had just got in. All this was, apparently, my fault!

It was perfect. I mean, if you're going to have a good season, why not do it in style? If you'd have asked me before the season started what was the ideal way to see Millwall win promotion I would have definitely gone for the 'late title-winning run denying Palace a play-off place in the process' option, but would never have been able to concoct something as delicious as the 'Whitney' story for the cherry on top. As schadenfreude goes it doesn't get any better. Fantastic.

Two weeks later I officially left school. We were of course due to return a few weeks later to sit our GCSEs – we were the first ones to take these new exams which replaced O levels. I walked out of the school gates for the final time as a pupil with the mandatory autograph book which was intended to be scribbled with well-wishing message from friends. Mine was mostly full of insults from embittered Palace fans – but there was also a note from Mr Green, my Middlesbrough-supporting English teacher. It read:

"Up one year, down the next – the vicissitudes of football. Good luck, Pete Green"

Vicissitudes. That was another word I'd have to look up.

13
AFTER THE LORD MAYOR'S SHOW

Throughout the weeks when Millwall kept winning, kept being awarded penalties and seemed to be edging miraculously, relentlessly toward their 103-year goal of First Division football we were paranoid. It's another football-supporting health hazard. Every day rationale is abandoned the minute you attach yourself and all of your emotions to a football team. It was too good to be true, little old Millwall going up? To the First Division? No, some sod would put a spanner in the works even if the players didn't mess it up. The most popular theory was that we'd end up in the play-offs and win them, only for the second leg of the final to be marred by crowd trouble and allow the football authorities the joyous decision of awarding the tie to the opposition as our punishment.

Ernie, ever the optimist, suggested that, even after the final whistle had blown on that final game, someone, somewhere, would come up with a way to stop us playing a season of First Division football. He was almost right.

Football was changing. In the relatively short time I had been following it, there had been a slow but steady transformation. The perception of it as a spectator sport had gone from being one level above train spotting to a genuine passion again. Various initiatives such as Sunday football and the play-offs had rekindled interest in the game. The hooligan problem, which seemed to reach a depressingly horrifying peak in 1985 appeared to be receding. As the fans came back, so did the interest from the television companies. The heady days of the 1970s when Match of the Day and its ITV counterpart were regular weekend staples were long gone. TV companies were in dispute with the game, leading to a total blackout at one point in 1986. Hard to imagine today.

Gregg Dyke at ITV had a plan. He knew that the real money was at the top of the game. The 'big ten'. The likes of Liverpool, Everton, Spurs, Manchester United. They were the hot ticket. With TV rights up for grabs and Rupert Murdoch entering the bidding war, Dyke had the brainwave of making his £47 million offer to the privileged few who were most likely to offer a return on the investment. The big ten had their heads turned. To quote Gordon Gekko from the hit film of the time: "Greed is good".

The proposals were for a 'breakaway league' of ten clubs who would get the big ITV cheque. Fans would be treated to regular live league matches of Liverpool v Manchester United, Arsenal v Spurs etc. Where did this leave Millwall? It left them out in the cold, of course. At one point the chairmen of the big ten clubs were preparing to submit their notice to leave the Football League and set up their new football utopia, leaving the other 82 clubs to fight over the scraps.

For about three weeks, my dream had been completely shattered. Millwall it seemed would be starting the following season pretty much right back where they had started 12 months before: with their nose pressed up against the glass watching on with envy at the biggest names in football that they should have been playing against. All we now had to look forward to was games against Coventry and Norwich. It felt like being shown 'what you could've won' on Bullseye.

Mercifully the negotiations fell apart. A big factor in this was the squabbling over exactly who this big ten should be with various clubs laying claim to the last few places based on either historical significance or recent lofty top flight finishes. As the big ten bitched, ITV realised their Super League plans were scuppered – for now – and a compromise was reached that saw twenty First Division clubs start the 1988-89 English Football League season – including Millwall. We'd made it. Again.

Only when I was finally able to pour over those magical fixtures did it really sink in. I had to confess at being a little disappointed at the first three: Aston Villa away and then Derby at home followed by Charlton away. We'd obviously played and beaten Villa twice during our promotion season, Derby had gone up just the season before and Charlton the year before that, so it wouldn't feel like arriving in the big time, more like a lap of honour. At least it might provide us with a steady start, a few points on the board before the big boys arrived.

Everton would be our first 'proper' First Division match at The Den. The same Everton that had just broken the British transfer record to sign West Ham's Tony Cottee. Then there would be established top flight names like Coventry and Nottingham Forest before the dream trip to Anfield to play Liverpool; Newcastle then West Ham, Spurs, Manchester United and then Arsenal – then we'd go around and play them all again. It was head spinning stuff and I couldn't wait.

The reality was though that all these stellar names were mere sideshows to the real achievement which was much more personal, so much closer to home and far more special. The real beauty of standing on those crumbling Den terraces, the same broken steps that we had trodden to see our team stumble against the likes of Chesterfield, Bury and Northampton just a few short seasons before, was that not only would I now be stood there with friends I had made along the way, but next to me would be the person responsible for this beautiful obsession, this love supreme, this mad, mad thing that compels grown men to dance unashamedly to celebrate and worship the action of other grown men, this Millwall: My dad.

We'd had our differences, and life was far from perfect, but for those precious hours on Saturday afternoons and Tuesday or Wednesday evenings, perfect is exactly what it was.

He said he'd never live to see the day when Millwall were in the First Division and, not for the first time, I was so glad to see him proved wrong.

"Right, Villa away then Dad?"

"Villa? Oh go on then."

Like I said earlier, *After The Lord Mayor's Show* was a phrase that used to puzzle me when I heard my mum or dad using it, but just a few years of following Millwall taught me exactly what it meant. Watching Millwall in the First Division was, of course, completely wonderful, everything the fans had dreamed of- and much more. At first anyway.

I promised I wouldn't dwell too much on statistics, but the first six matches of that historic season deserve to be dissected a little.

We roared into a 2-0 lead at Villa and despite being pegged back to 2-2 were confident that Derby would pose us few problems at The Den. We were right, and in true fairy tale tradition, I stood on the terraces with my dad and my best friends in the glorious sunshine and watched my beloved Lions win their first ever top flight match.

The sun was still shining a week later when we thrashed Charlton 3-0 and even the rain couldn't dampen our spirits as we beat Everton with relative ease 2-1 back at The Den. This was the same Everton team that had won two league titles in the previous three years, along with FA Cup and European success, yet we appeared to roll them over just as we had so many teams in our run to the title a few months before, it was bizarre, but I was living in absolute football Nirvana.

It was as if the momentum that had taken us to the top of the Second Division was just continuing to build with every game. Even falling behind twice at Norwich the following week didn't knock us off our stride, on both occasions we equalised within a minute of the home side scoring. Going into that match Norwich were early season league leaders and Millwall were third. THIRD - IN THE FIRST DIVISION! We were battling it out with

Norwich to be the champions of English football for crying out loud – where would this end?

The media were already talking about the likelihood of Millwall emulating Ipswich's feat when they won the 1960-61 Second Division title and followed it up with the league title in 1962. It was funny how the tabloids had suddenly warmed to us, after all the years of either completely ignoring us or grossly exaggerating the slightest incident and splashing it across the front pages, they suddenly seemed to love us. It doesn't do it any justice, but I can only describe it as the most surreal feeling ever. It was pure exhilaration, it coloured my entire life, I was literally walking on air and everything seemed to go right - simply flowing along in Millwall's success slipstream. Looking back it was a bit like one of those Jim Carrey films where he says yes to everything or can't lie.

I'd started college and it was a doddle, my timetable allowed me loads of free time, I'd also started working part time at the local Sainsbury's. Student workers had to work Saturdays, it was compulsory as it was their busiest day. This wasn't a problem during the summer but as the season approached there was no way I'd be sat at a checkout or lumping boxes of soap powder around the warehouse while Millwall were playing. I was taking every bit of overtime they could throw at me and saving like mad, in the unlikely event I'd have enough money to finance all Millwall matches through a jobless season. It was obvious I'd have nowhere near enough. With a week to go before the season started I approached Julian, the store assistant manager, and told him that I'd have to leave as I was starting college soon and my parents wanted me to spend the weekends studying for my A Levels. What a joke that was, my folks didn't even take enough interest to know what subjects I'd taken at college let alone compel me to spend every Saturday and Sunday with my head in my books!

Luckily, I had made myself pretty indispensable. I was one of the few students he could rely on to do the awful Sunday overtime shift and, in his words, one of the few that "wasn't a total fuckwit". I had also found myself in the company football team. I told you everything seemed to be going my way. As I said, I was, at best, an average player but when it came to trials for the team and then matches against our fellow branches in a tournament that would see the final played at Selhurst Park, everything just seemed to click, I was playing right back and cruising through games. Not wanting to lose either a valuable member of staff or the team, Julian said he'd sort something out, and he did.

My weekends were free and I now worked Tuesday evenings – which was a doddle because the store was dead – as well as Thursdays and Fridays. My new hours actually boosted my pay up to over £60 a week. I truly had the Midas touch – or the Millwall touch.

It was hard to believe how things could get better, but they did.

On the first day of October 1988 the sun shone across The Den as we took our places on the terraces to watch Millwall take on QPR. It wasn't the most keenly anticipated of London derbies, QPR were a bit like Brentford or Fulham to us, there was little real rivalry with our neighbours from west of the capital for some reason. Rangers were however a well-established top flight team and it would prove another good test of our top flight credentials. We were still nestled nicely in third place, although deep down none of us were really imagining that we could keep this up for the whole season, we were just enjoying it while it lasted.

That match will live long in the memory of Millwall supporters forever for many reasons, but I'll guarantee that I can name two of them. The atmosphere around the place was like a celebratory last match of the season and a season opener all rolled into one. It was something The Den had seemed to have perfected that season so far. It was a carnival atmosphere with a subtle blend of arrogance, invincibility and of course the menace that only The Den could provide which meant that many teams were beaten almost as soon as they took to the pitch.

I don't care what anyone says, you simply cannot fabricate that.

When I read about some of the efforts clubs and fans make to 'create' a great atmosphere at football – especially in the Premier League and all-seater era, I find myself cringing. Singing areas, drums, trumpets, clappers, pre-rehearsed songs, outfits and banners with pithy or pro-fan political statements, it's all crap, it's fake, I hate it, and it's not what following football is about. It certainly wasn't in 1988.

During Euro 96 I was watching England v Scotland in a beer garden in Manchester. The IRA had bombed the local Arndale Centre that morning. I had been travelling in to the city centre to meet some friends to watch the match when it went off. After spending an hour or so stuck on a hot train I eventually made it to the pub. Watching with us was a group of German fans who were in the city for their match against Russia at Old Trafford the following day.

Following the mayhem of the penalty save and Gazza's fantastic goal, the Germans seemed to be even more excitable about England than we were. After the game, I chatted with them over a few post-match pints and they explained that English football was deeply envied amongst fans right across Germany. They loved the passion and the spontaneity and couldn't get their heads around it, but absolutely loved everything about it. It's such a shame that 1996 was the year that the English game really started to lose that uniqueness about it.

Mention the 1988 Millwall v QPR match to any Millwall fan who was there and I can assure you one name will instantly leave their lips:

Terry Hurlock.

Hurlock was already a favourite at The Den. How could he not be? But this match was surely the pinnacle of his Lions career.

Everything was going to plan as usual and Millwall led through an early Cascarino header. Then, Rangers player-manager Trevor Francis, who had been mercilessly jibed about his similarity to comedian Jasper Carrot from the first whistle temporarily silenced The Den with an equaliser from nothing in the 30th minute and for a very short while after that goal Millwall appeared to be rattled for the first time in months.

QPR sensed some frailty and went for a second goal, the fans were starting to get a little restless as the usually efficient Millwall midfield started to concede possession cheaply and Rangers came close to a second goal. Millwall were in desperate need of someone to regain control of the game, to grab it by the scruff of the neck. Cometh the hour, cometh the man.

As QPR started to build another attack from midway in their own half, Hurlock chased down the Rangers defender who panicked and attempted to play the ball back to his 'keeper, Hurlock continued his rampaging run and made it to the ball first before calmly playing it across to Cascarino for his and Millwall's second.

Ninety seconds later in an almost identical situation, the same Rangers defender again found himself in possession with the terrifying sight of Hurlock bearing down on him. This time, once he had won the ball there was only one thing on his mind and he let fly from 20 yards to make it 3-1 and send the crowd into absolute delirium.

QPR nicked another in the second half but the score finished 3-2 and as results came in from other grounds following the final whistle, it quickly became apparent that the other memory that all Lions fans there that day would take to their graves was that October 1st 1988 would be the day that little old Millwall sat proudly at the top of the 92 English Football League clubs.

I remembered my dad's story about Preston at home back in 1972, when incorrect reports of scores elsewhere had thousands of Millwall supporters celebrating promotion to the First Division – only for the stadium announcer to reveal the brutal reality that it wasn't to be.

Dad had to wait another 16 years for that memory to be erased, and here we were, together, on the sun-bathed crumbling concrete of the Millwall terraces, just standing there while every other fan made their way to the exits to start the celebrations in the local pubs. We just looked at each other, with huge childish grins on our faces, our feet seemed frozen to the spot. Dad's eyes were glazing over.

He was never one to show emotion, but, in that tiny, perfect moment, the kind that you wish you could save forever and revisit physically rather than just in the fading memory, I think he shed a tear. A tear for all the years he had waited to see his team in the First Division. He'd have happily accepted losing every game and going straight back down I think, but here we were, on top of the lot.

I tried to find some words, but found myself paralysed with the emotion of it all. It almost felt like it wasn't my place to say anything. It would have been fitting if Dad had found something poignant to sum up the moment, but that wasn't Dad's thing. Finally, with the ground virtually empty and the sun finally starting to dip down behind the roof of the stand he finally broke the silence:

"Come on son, look at the time, Mum'll do her nut…"

While the Millwall machine seemed to keep on rolling, our lofty position was to only last a fortnight. A goalless draw at Coventry saw us back in second spot and we really wobbled at home to Nottingham Forest when we had to stage a late comeback from 2-0 down to draw with Cloughie's boys and our first defeat of the season came in typically Millwall-like style – away to one of the teams that had been promoted with us – at Middlesbrough.

A 2-2 draw at Southampton looked good on paper. The south coast team were, along with Millwall and Norwich, the surprise top three of the season so far, but it felt like the last drop of rocket fuel had been used up and while we would continue our upward arc for a few months more, there was a distinct feeling that the good times were finally on the wane.

Millwall were still in the top three at the end of March, but from then, four draws and six defeats saw them finish tenth. There was a palpable feeling of deflation around the place again as well as a realisation that, in truth, the First Division could actually be quite boring!

14
LIFE IS WHAT HAPPENS...

When I was 14 I, like many boys my age, had a morning paper round. Sunday was pay day and as I walked in to collect my week's wages one September morning, I saw Sanjay the shopkeeper pulling some exciting looking boxes from a larger brown cardboard box on the floor. They were football stickers.

The new Panini Football 87 album was out – and here were the first batch of stickers. I loved collecting them, but like the millions who did the same, always found myself frustrated at the end of the season with a tatty album, pages falling lose from their staples and gaps I could not fill – no matter how many swaps I did in the school playground, and there always seemed to be three or four too many to send off for using the little form in the back of the album.

"Guess what's in here?" Sanjay purred as he tapped the small carton of Football 87 stickers.

"Er, stickers obviously Sanj" I replied

"Ah no, more than that Merv, this one box will fill the whole Football 87 album".

According to Sanjay, the way it worked was that a carton of stickers had every one required to fill the album, but as nobody actually bought an entire carton – just a handful from it – that was why they never filled it. I doubted this for a few minutes but couldn't control my curiosity.

Minutes later I arrived home, having swapped my week's wages for the carton of stickers. I spent the entire afternoon feverishly ripping them from their wrappers and carefully placing them in their appropriate space in the album.

Sanjay was true to his word. By the time I'd finished I was surrounded by about 700 curled sticker backs, torn wrappers, about half a dozen or so doubles and an immaculate, fully complete edition of Panini Football 87. For a few seconds I was beside myself with joy, a childhood ambition fulfilled. Then it hit me.

In my desperation to complete the perfect Panini album I had sacrificed months of fun and anticipation in buying a few packets of stickers on my way to school, spotting the odd shiny and swapping with mates. It was *too perfect*, I realised how much I actually liked the frustration and fruitlessness of it and now I had lost that forever.

I tossed the album to one side, binned the gloomy detritus of months of wasted fun and never picked up a sticker book again, even when Millwall finally appeared in it two years later for the first time as a First Division team.

I don't think it works like that with the stickers these days but it taught me a valuable lesson, although one which I'd always been aware of in the back of my mind. When I used to listen to Wizard's *I Wish It Could Be Christmas Every Day* as a young child, I quickly thought this through and realised that, as great as that sounds, it would spoil the excitement of the event somewhat and I was quite content with having to wait another twelve months.

Millwall in the First Division quickly became a novelty with all the shelf life of one of those cracker toys. We'd squeezed a lifetime of First Division joy into about three quarters of one season. We'd been top of the league, been ahead at Anfield, visited Old Trafford, Highbury, White Hart Lane and Goodison and while we'd look forward to going to those places again the following season, it just wasn't the same. In fact, as melodramatic as it sounds, supporting Millwall was never the same for me again.

Despite another brief flirtation with top spot after a 4-0 win over Coventry in September, the tricky second season proved to be just that. A home win over Aston Villa in December was the last and Millwall were relegated ignominiously in April. Just as I had been at Hull to see us win promotion, I watched our First Division days end at Derby, but it was all taken in good humour. For the months when relegation was just a matter of time, Millwall fans sang about the Football League being upside down and seemed almost chipper about their impending life back in the second tier.

Things changed very quickly, for Millwall and for me. The club had clearly not made the money that they had hoped from that first season and there were rumours of player unrest over contracts. Cascarino was sold to Aston Villa and his replacement Paul Goddard became the club's record signing – and a total disaster. Desperate to improve finances, the club floated on the stock exchange allowing fans to buy shares in their club, and then invested in a doomed pub chain which plunged the club deeper in the mire. Millwall had flourished in the big time doing it their way – now they were trying to behave like one of the big boys and making a right mess of it.

I still loved going to as many games as I could, but with relegation in 1990 came some changes for me too – and when I least expected them.

I left a payphone on a side street in Blackpool where I was on holiday with Steve and a couple of other friends after calling Dad to find out the fixtures for the new Second Division season which had just been published and took the short walk to the nearest pub to discuss with Steve our Millwall trips for the new campaign. The sting of relegation hadn't lasted long and there were plenty of new away trips to look forward to - which would include plans to fly to our September away match at Newcastle, just for a change to the usual coach or train, as long as the aircraft was in better shape than that coach we took to Leicester three years before.

As we sipped our first pints, I noticed a blonde girl sat at the other side of the pub. Steve was usually the one to make advances in pubs and embarrass us both, but on this occasion I decided I wanted to make a move. We agreed to finish our pints first so we could make a quick exit after the expected rebuff but to my surprise my offer of a drink was accepted with a friendly smile and Steve repeated the offer to her friend.

That was it. In about ten minutes I'd gone from making plans to spend the next nine months following Millwall all over the country and writing the next chapter of my football following life story, to meeting Anna, my future wife and mother of my three children.

As John Lennon said: "*Life is what happens while you're busy making other plans*", and, for the first time in my life, something took the place of Millwall.

Anna was from Stockport and for 18 months or so I fitted weekend visits around Millwall home matches by getting an early Sunday morning train, away games were ditched altogether and soon I was conspicuous by my absence on Den terraces, catching a train straight from work on Friday and spending the weekend with Anna. She would visit me one weekend each month and we'd take in a game – yes, it was *my* turn to break the 'no birds at the match' rule. Things were moving fast.

Early one Wednesday morning the phone rang. This wasn't unusual. My mum's work would sometimes call at around 6am to confirm her shifts for the day so, still half asleep, I let it ring, only for my mum to burst in to my room with the phone in her hand. "It's for you", she said, looking puzzled.

It was Anna's mum. Anna had gone into labour. I didn't know. Nobody did. She had managed to conceal the pregnancy from everyone but now the time had come when she couldn't keep it a secret any longer. A few hours later she gave birth to a baby boy, I was on the train to Stockport, but by the time I arrived and held my son for the first time, Anna had become very ill.

Not long after the birth, Anna complained of feeling unwell, with severe headaches. Soon after she started fitting – the symptoms of postpartum preeclampsia. She was moved to another hospital in Manchester where she was given drugs to put her in an induced coma to stop the convulsions. By that evening, doctors were telling us her chances of survival were 70-30 against her pulling through. Thankfully, after two days she responded to treatment and made a full recovery.

Our son still didn't have a name. It was a late Saturday afternoon and Anna's parents arrived for visiting. Keen to inject a bit of levity, but in my usual clumsy, inappropriate, football-obsessed manner, I joked that if Teddy Sheringham had scored for Millwall that day we'd be calling our new addition 'Teddy'. I say joked because we were playing Leicester away, a venue where, through my own personal experience, we never did well so didn't think there was much chance anyway. As Anna's dad took his seat next to her bed I asked him if he knew the Millwall score.

"Won 2-1" came his reply.

"Who scored?" I enquired, glancing at Anna who was giving me the first showing of a look I would come to recognise in the years to follow.

"Sheringham got both" he said.

I turned to Anna, but before I could get the words out, she hit me with a very firm: "NO!", and, for the first time during that traumatic week, we found reason to laugh. In the end we settled for Michael. One of the nurses that had cared for Anna that week had remarked about my London accent, saying that her boyfriend Michael was also from London. After failing to agree on a whole list of names, that one seemed just right.

In April 1992 I watched my last Millwall home game as a London resident, before moving to live in Stockport with Anna and Michael. Millwall were getting ready for their final season at The Den having built a brand new all-seater stadium. Suddenly everything had changed.

I was 19, Anna was 17. We were still kids and yet here we were, with a child of our own, and a mortgage, it was quite terrifying if you stopped to think about it. So we didn't. We just got on with it.

Suddenly, not only was I seeing life from a completely different angle, but my view of my own dad totally changed. I could instantly relate to the pressure of providing for your family and see how being a dad could get lost in the day to day routine. I was determined to do things differently.

I still managed visits to matches – but they were few and far between and dictated by finances and family always came first. I have to admit to missing being there almost every match. Occasional weekend visits to Mum and Dad almost always took in a Millwall home match. The day my son was born I imagined taking him to his first football match and watching him playing for his local junior team – a lot of presumptions, but thankfully ones that I was able to fulfil with both my boys. It wasn't quite as I had imagined it back in the days on The Den terraces.

I can remember when I stood I front of my dad resting on the crush barrier and, if there was a big crowd, he'd lift me up to get a better view when the action came close. Soon, I was joined by Steve and Stuart and our dads – none of whom stood more than five foot six in height - were now the ones standing in front of us. We used to joke about picking them up to see better and talk about how it wouldn't be long before it was our own sons stood in front of them and completing three generations of Millwall support. Like I said, a lot was being presumed.

Four years after Michael was born, we had another son who we named Tom. Well, Thomas Edward to be exact – that was as close as I was going to get to naming any of our children 'Teddy'.

The reality was that I did take my sons to The Den, but this time we were sat on a shiny blue seat in a new purpose-built stadium and there was never any chance of them becoming hooked and Millwall regulars in the way I had as soon as Dad took me.

I instead discovered a new football world that was just as thrilling and fulfilling as following Millwall – being a football dad. For fifteen years I drove all over the north west and stood ankle deep in mud in wind, rain, hail and snow watching them from the age of five to seventeen compete at various levels of the game. There were times when both played on the same day at the same time and it killed me to miss watching one of them, I was determined to follow their junior footballing adventures after being so disappointed at how my own dad had virtually ignored mine. Football had once again provided a bond between father and son, but I didn't just stop there and it extended to music, films, TV programmes, in fact any common ground that I could find I grasped with both hands. I wasn't going to leave my sons to do all the legwork when it came to my relationship with my sons.

Dad of course continued to renew his season ticket – and emptily threaten to bin it after every bad game. It certainly wasn't the same following The Lions together with 200 miles between us, but Saturday evening phone calls and match reports carefully cut out of the local South London Press newspaper and mailed to me each week along with the match programme papered over the cracks a little. Dad was a proud man and, apart from shedding a tear the day I left south London for good, he never let on about how he was feeling. Mum would often say how sad he looked when he set off for matches on his own, and no matter how much I told him to catch up with the old gang, he insisted on sitting alone at matches.

When I look back at how it all panned out it's quite bizarre, almost as if, by seeing Millwall finally win promotion to the First Division alongside Dad it was mission accomplished, but that goes against everything that football gives us – a new season, a fresh start, a chance to regain higher league status, an opportunity for more glory. Yet I felt strangely fulfilled and whilst I did miss the week in week out visits to matches at times, there was a feeling of completion and closure about it, almost like when a couple admit that a relationship has run its course and have the courage to go their separate ways.

I suppose what we were both thinking in that silence after the QPR match when we had gone to the top of the league, was: "Well, how do you top that?" When you're at the very top, there is only one way you can go really.

But there was some unfinished business. We had still never seen Millwall at Wembley, or in an FA Cup final. If you'd have been able to grant me three footballing wishes when I boarded that train at Euston on the day I left home they would have been to go back in time and make sure Dad was with me at Hull on the day we won promotion and to share with him a trip to Wembley and an FA Cup final appearance. At the time I probably could have killed the last two birds with one stone, but as it transpired, fate smiled on us twice more.

In 1999 Millwall won through to the final of the Auto Windscreens Shield – at Wembley. I sat with Dad and Mike, my eldest who was eight at the time, as fifty thousand Millwall fans celebrated the club's first ever official visit to the famous twin towers (the 1944 War Time FA Cup against Chelsea there definitely doesn't count) and in typical Millwall fashion, we lost to a last minute goal to a Wigan side that we had already beaten twice in the league that season.

Twelve months later the old stadium was demolished in preparation for the new one, we had managed to watch Millwall at Wembley at just about the last possible opportunity – it would certainly be the last chance for Dad anyway.

Then in 2004 the unimaginable happened: Millwall reached the FA Cup final. In a cup run that provided no sterner challenge than Walsall, Telford, Burnley and Tranmere, we found ourselves in the nosebleed territory of an FA Cup semi-final – against fellow second tier side Sunderland, managed quite ironically by ex Millwall manager Mick McCarthy. The venue for the tie couldn't have been better: Old Trafford – a fifteen minute drive from our home. I sat with Dad and both of my sons as we watched history made on the fourth day of the fourth month in 2004 –a 1-0 victory courtesy of a goal from Tim Cahill – our number four.

When I sat down to watch my first ever FA Cup at home final way back in 1980 the fans' rendition of *'Abide With Me'* sent a shiver down my eight-year-old spine. I couldn't work out why. In all the years that hymn was sung in the traditional way at the cup final, it always had the same effect as I watched on television. It's a tradition that was sadly never truly kept with the brass band marching slowly in time over the Wembley turf. But even in its more modern format, as the first chords began on that May day at Cardiff's Millennium Stadium and we began to sing that same hymn together before *our* team played in the FA Cup final, I looked to my left at my two sons and to my right at my dad and very nearly completely lost it.

Just like that sunny October afternoon in 1988, there wasn't really anywhere we could go from here. It was perfect, we had done it all.

There was one brand new Millwall experience which was provided courtesy of that FA Cup final appearance which unfortunately we were not able to share first hand though. Despite the comprehensive 3-0 defeat to Manchester United, we found ourselves qualifying for Europe by virtue of the fact that United had already claimed one of the places in the following season's Champions League, leaving the UEFA Cup place which was awarded to the FA Cup winners in the hands of little old Millwall. You had to laugh. After spending over 100 years waiting to play in the First Division and becoming the last London club to do so, we had now qualified for European competition – a feat that only a few can ever dream of.

A two-legged defeat to Hungary's Ferencvaros meant that Millwall's European adventure was short-lived and it only served to provide a distraction as the inevitable decline began again.

After following the club for so long you became finely tuned to spotting it. Good players left for better things (Tim Cahill moving to Everton for a paltry £1.5 million) and were replaced inadequately. Results and league position start to dip and what we thought would be an inevitable climb into the Premier League for the first time to complement our FA Cup and European exploits never happened.

We prepared ourselves for bleaker times ahead, but dark clouds were gathering much closer to home for Dad.

After Christmas 2006, with Millwall hurtling back towards the third tier of English football, Dad was taken to hospital where x-rays showed fluid on his lungs. An appointment was made for a CT Scan and I travelled down to their home in Kent to accompany him on the Friday, he was understandably petrified, knowing exactly what the scans were trying to diagnose.

In an attempt to raise his spirits we went to The Den the following day to watch a home game with fellow strugglers Leicester. The entire day panned out as a complete mirror image to that glorious sunny autumn day back in 1979 when we watched Millwall together for the first time. A bleak, grey, drizzly March afternoon saw a feeble performance greeted by hoots of derision from the home fans and groans of resignation as Leicester ran out unconvincing 1-0 winners. Almost three decades after Dad had taken me to my first Millwall match, I had taken him to his last.

Soon after Dad was diagnosed with Mesothelioma, an incurable form of cancer linked to asbestos, which the consultants believed he had come into contact with during his days as a builder. He was told he'd probably have six to nine months.

By October Mum and Dad were preparing to leave Kent after buying a bungalow five minutes away from our house, I was desperately trying to find some positive energy to throw at it while Dad's had completely drained away. Finally, everything was in place, a move date set and, a week before that, an appointment to discuss starting Dad's chemo.

The Neil Cliffe Centre at Wythenshawe in south Manchester sits in the grounds of the main Wythenshawe Hospital. A relatively new building, its bright brickwork and shiny new paint illuminate it against the dour old lines of its landlord. It specialises in the diagnosis and treatments of cancers and serious conditions associated with the lungs – but other life-limiting conditions are also covered. It's hardly the kind of brochure write-up anyone would enjoy reading and should certainly make it into the top ten places you'd hope never to have to visit – either as a patient, or family member of one.

My first reaction when we parked the car and paid for our ticket as made our way to the entrance was the irony of it being next door to the main hospital's maternity section. Over the coming months we would cross paths with many expectant fathers and mums-to-be racing into the double doors of the delivery suites awaiting the arrival of new life as we trudged on past them, round to the rear of the building and into the dimly-lit low-level Neil Cliffe centre trying to support Dad clinging on to his.

After five months of tests, prodding and poking, radiotherapy and a house move from Hell, we sat outside the consultant's office waiting for what we hoped would be the start of an upturn in fortunes. This new chemotherapy treatment that was only available here could give Dad three to five years instead of the nine months that he had been offered when his cancer was diagnosed back in May. It was October now, the clock was ticking and very much against us.

The meeting we were told was a formality but essential prior to a patient being accepted for chemotherapy. The consultant would first speak to all of us and then my dad alone. As the consultant explained how would it all work Dad sat staring at the floor, Mum tried hard to take it in through glazed eyes and I did my best to nod at the right places and ask what I thought were sensible questions. Mum and I then retook our seats outside and Dad was left with the consultant.

"We'll only be about ten" he mouthed as he closed the door.

Just under two hours later the door slowly opened and Dad appeared. He looked awful. As if he'd run a marathon – but without the sweat. He looked at me with what felt like a guilty apologetic expression – as if he'd done something that had got me into trouble.

The consultant, now looking a little less relaxed than he had done when we first met him, beckoned me in.

"Can I have a word? Your mum can stay with your dad".

I followed him into his office, puzzled not only about the reason for being called back in, but the length of time he had spent with my dad. I didn't have long to wait. He came straight out with it:

"Your father is clinically depressed".

After months of being asked how my terminally ill dad was by well-meaning friends, it was a conundrum I was used to dealing with. Inside I would reply: "Well he was told he's got nine months to live in May, it's now August, how do you think he's getting on?" Outwardly I had perfected several eloquent versions of "as well as can be expected".

So my inward reaction to this diagnosis was: "No shit Sherlock, can't imagine what he's got to feel down about can you?"

The consultant could clearly see I was struggling with a response and picked up on the signals.

"This is not just about his cancer. Your father has been depressed for many years." He elaborated.

I couldn't work out why he was suddenly referring to him as my 'father' all of a sudden. He was 'Dad' a moment ago?

"I don't get it" was all I could respond with, but deep down I had a feeling what was coming.

"It appears to stem back to the time when he lost his own father, losing his job, money problems, among other things. He's also admitted to contemplating suicide. I asked him some standard questions that we ask all patients being considered for chemotherapy and it all came out."

He paused, and then added what felt like a little disclaimer:

"Of course, this doesn't constitute a formal diagnosis but all the signs are there"

This completely hit me for six. It all came out? Really? From my dad? The man who never shared his innermost thoughts or fears with anyone?

Gradually it all started to make sense. The mood swings, the silences, the obsession with tidiness, and of course, when I heard him muttering: "I feel like doing myself in". It was right there in front of us, but just like him, we covered it up, tried to hide it and just get on with life. We kidded ourselves it wasn't there because we couldn't see it, but, just like his cancer, it was growing slowly but surely for over four decades and eventually there was no hiding from it any more.

Deep down, if we were being completely honest, we knew something was wrong, properly wrong but we simply didn't have the knowledge to recognise exactly what it was or the courage to attempt to confront it.

Despite these revelations, the consultant was happy to allow my dad to undergo chemotherapy, although that final decision still needed to be carefully considered and taken by him based on what we had been told.

We made our way back to the car park in silence, passing two heavily pregnant women sat on the wall at the entrance to the Maternity ward chatting animatedly and dragging heavily on their cigarettes. It was the sort of scene that my mum would not usually have been able to resist passing judgement on, and would have always elicited an old-fashioned look at the culprits followed by a long holier-than-thou tirade, straight off the editorial pages of The Daily Mail for the duration of our fifteen minute journey home. This time however there was nothing, just silence.

The chemotherapy was intended to extend Dad's life, but it didn't. On Thursday, February 1st 2007, eight months after his condition was diagnosed, Dad passed away. He was 68. He'd easily surpassed that 51 target I had set for him back in my teens, but that was little consolation. Those two decades seemed to have vanished in the blink of an eye. Two days later, still feeling numb, I took my radio from its usual place on the kitchen windowsill and placed it on a small table in the centre of our lounge. I switched it to Five Live and sat listening as the scores from all over the country were relayed back by various correspondents. The television remained switched off. As I sat and took in the first 90 minutes of football without my dad, I couldn't help but raise a smile as news of Millwall's 1-0 win away at Yeovil came through. Yeovil? We *never* win there! I managed to stay relatively composed right up until 'Out of the Blue' struck up for Sports Report and the reading of the final scores, then tears streamed down my cheeks as James Alexander Gordon read the days results and I was transported back to that walk from The Den with Dad as we gave chase to Radio Man.

Later that evening I sat at my computer and resolved to write the eulogy for my dad's funeral service. I wanted everyone present to know that, whilst he was far from the perfect Dad, as I was nowhere near a perfect son, our less-than-perfect relationship had blossomed into something really special – even if it was only seemingly held together by the flimsiest of ties: football.

The piece went on for pages and pages and I quickly realised it was going to be far too long, but I couldn't stop myself and it all just flowed out of me.

When it was done I posted it on The House of Fun – a Millwall supporters' forum that I had been a member of for the past few years. I wanted to share with my fellow Millwall fans what Millwall meant to me, but more importantly why.

It was never about chasing success or glory and there was never any question of turning our backs when things got tough, it was *our* team, with all its faults and imperfections, just as my relationship was with Dad.

In the months that followed my dad's death I found my relationship with Michael becoming increasingly strained. He was now the same rebellious age 15 that I had been back in 1987. He, very much like my dad, found it hard to open up and express his feelings and took Dad's passing badly. He was no longer playing football, I was feeling sorry for myself, and it soon became apparent that, for all my efforts not to make the same mistakes as my dad, history could easily repeat itself if I wasn't careful. It was a timely reminder that, as a dad, you can never take your eye off the ball – and that sometimes, football alone just isn't enough.

Shortly after Dad died we had our third child. A daughter. That broke a long history of boys on my side of the family. We named her Natasha and gave her a middle name of Victoria in memory of Dad. I was excited at the prospect of a new fatherhood challenge and made a promise to myself not to force football on her. It's a promise that I kept and whilst we share our passions for music among many other bonds, she cannot fathom my love for the beautiful game, which is fair enough.

Living in Manchester, with Manchester United-supporting in-laws, it's unfair to expect your sons to support anyone other than Manchester United. I had a job explaining to work colleagues and friends when I moved why I supported Millwall, in fact, even living in south London in the 1980s I found myself having to justify why I didn't support Chelsea, or even Liverpool or Manchester United – the choice of many of my school-friends. For me the answer was always simple and straightforward. Growing up, I took it for granted that I'd have sons and that my sons would follow in the family tradition of following Millwall. In the days of Sky Sports and the Premier League, their school friends would wonder why they supported Milllwall – and they'd say the same as me.

I accepted that would no longer be the case once I moved to Manchester and, even though those sons did come along exactly as I expected, and, like me, they became football-mad, I had to concede that, when asked who they supported, the anticipated reply of "United" would need no further justification.

That said, for all its glitz and glamour, the Premier League has nothing on

Oldham away on a cold, wet Saturday afternoon in November, and it only took a few away trips with my sons to make them realise that there was something very unique about this special little club.

Maybe it triggered something deep down in their genetic make-up, a Millwall gene perhaps, but there was certainly something there.

The modern game being what it is means that the sort of relationship I was able to forge with my dad through going to football is almost impossible these days. I'm sure there are lots of fathers and sons (and of course, fathers and daughters, mothers and sons etc) that go to every game and find their relationship enhanced by sharing the ups and downs of following their team, but only after investing hundreds, if not thousands of pounds in advance for season tickets. The spontaneity has gone, and with that, a big slice of the magic too.

So my sons, like many, have to content themselves with following their team mostly from an armchair or pub stool on Sky Sports. Only when they go with me to Millwall matches do they get a glimpse of the *real* game.

So I suppose there is some consolation in the fact that, as they have grown up, they have recognised the place Millwall has in their family tree, the importance of why that hastily organised trip on that September day back in 1979 meant so much. I'm grateful that, like me, they shun large parts of the modern game – the half and half scarves and all that rubbish – and that includes having "two teams".

I could never stand that expression growing up, when another kid would say he supported "Liverpool and Arsenal". These days, you find grown men who insist that they support their chosen team *and* Barcelona. No. No you don't. You definitely don't *support* Barcelona. Saturated television coverage paints the illusion for you that you can. In fact it has totally blurred the lines of what supporting a football team is. It is for that reason that I wouldn't expect either of my sons to say they support Manchester United *and* Millwall. Which they don't.

I still get asked the same question today, whether it's through work or chatting to my sons' friends or other dads on the school run who hear my accent for the first time and assume I'm either a Chelsea or Manchester United fan – the two obvious choices for a Londoner it seems.

"Millwall? Why Millwall?"

To which I reply: "Because my dad did".

Both of my sons are now grown men, and as keen players of the game can often be seen on the local five-a-side courts with their mates who are all wearing their mandatory red or sky blue United or City shirts. Standing out amongst these is the navy blue shirt won by my sons. It's always a talking point for any new-comers to a match and will elicit the same inquisitive glance at the badge wondering who the shirt is. Both will happily explain that while they're United fans, they like Millwall because their dad is from London and it's *his* team and he supported them because his dad, their granddad did. They'll often add that they go to a few Millwall matches and sometimes remind their inquisitor that Teddy Sheringham came from Millwall.

It's not how I imagined it growing up, but it'll do for me.

EPILOGUE – WHATEVER BECAME OF SPLODGEGUN?

I almost forgot, the Splodgegun story isn't quite complete. At least I'm fairly certain it isn't.

Late in 1984 I was out with a friend, looking for something to do on a boring Sunday afternoon. We had moved house the previous year, but only a couple of miles to the other side of South Norwood. At the back of our new house was an old disused quarry, known to locals as 'The Brickies'. It was just an expanse of wasteland with a large man-made lake, and could be accessed via the alleyway that ran down the back of our garden. I used to look at it from my bedroom window and watch fishermen climbing through a gap in the fence and dragging their angling gear through it after them before spending the day sat by the murky water. My friend suggested we go and explore it so, with no better ideas, I agreed and we were soon edging our way down the steep bank to the water's edge, hopeful of finding something interesting in the water as young boys do – an old car, some hastily stashed loot from a local bank robbery or jewellery shop raid perhaps? Of course we found nothing more than mud and an old shopping trolley but busied ourselves chucking stuff in the water for a few minutes until we were suddenly aware we had company.

"Alright?" chirped a familiar voice.

I looked up to the top of the embankment to see two older boys, one dark-haired, the other blonde. I instantly recognised the dark-haired boy but just couldn't put a name to his face or voice. Despite the fact that I recognised him, I felt uneasy about the situation. Perhaps sensing my distrust, the dark-haired boy smiled, repeated his greeting and then explained that they were looking for a dog and would we help them. My suspicion increased, it was an unconvincing performance and I couldn't shake the fact that I recognised him.

"I'm sorry we can't, we've got to be home in a minute" I replied, trying not to show the increasing fear that something wasn't right about this. I was quickly proved right as the situation suddenly turned.

Now the blonde boy took over, he made his way down the steep embankment and shoved my friend, sending him stumbling back towards the water, he managed to stop himself from going right in, falling to his side, his left hand planted in the muddy water. As the blonde boy moved towards him my friend started to sob. I looked at the dark-haired boy, expecting it to be my turn next. I looked him I the eye and I noticed his face change, as if he too recognised me, then both of us turned to see the blonde boy who had now picked up a large piece of wood and was making his way towards my now hysterical friend who was pleading for him not to do anything. I looked back at the dark-haired boy and once again felt that frustrating sense of us recognising each other but not being able to put a name to the face.

"Leave it" he shouted and walked over to the blonde boy and snatched the wood from his hand, tossing it into the lake. "Let's go". And with that they made their way back up the embankment and off around to the other side of the lake. I helped my friend up and we quickly clambered through the hole in the fence and back down the alley to the main road.

My friend, still sobbing, also sensed that I knew the dark-haired boy, which appeared to have saved us, but I just couldn't work out why he seemed so familiar and yet nameless. A few weeks later as I was going over the episode again it suddenly clicked. I was as sure as I could be that it was Rob, Spartan Royals captain and Splodgegun sidekick.

I'd completely forgotten about the incident until one morning some time in 2011 when I was idly Googling stuff and found details of a book by the psychic Tony Stockwell. A name jumped out at me from the search results: Reece Collins. Reece had gone to the same primary school as me but was two years older. I didn't know him to talk to, but I knew of him. He was a popular boy and had loads of friends. In 1985 he'd been found hanged on wasteland near his home, he was just fifteen. An inquest at the time returned a verdict of suicide, which his parents weren't happy with as there were numerous pieces of evidence that pointed to foul play and involvement form another party. The most significant of this was that the belt used to hang him wasn't his and there was no traces of the algae from the tee on his body which there would have been if he had climbed it unaided. Three years after that verdict their campaigning paid off when a new enquiry was launched and an open verdict recorded.

Stockwell was invited by Reece's dad Roy to do a reading for them, but he uncovered far more than any of them could have bargained for – and as I read what he believed happened to Reece I was shocked to the core.

Stockwell claimed to see Reece walking along and seeing someone he knew, this person asked him if would help him to find a missing dog in the local woods and Reece duly obliged.

When the psychic and Reece's parents visited the spot close to where his dad found him hanging, Stockwell said he could sense the presence of an older man at the time, a man who was teased a lot by kids and that he wore a long rain coat – a trench coat even. He went on to explain that once this man began to attack Reece another man arrived to prevent him from struggling.

This was in 1985, a year after we'd been asked by those two boys to help them find a dog.

Stockwell then goes on to describe another case, the disappearance of 16-year-old Kevin Hicks who lived just a mile or so from me. Hicks left his home in March 1986 to buy ingredients for a school cookery lesson and was never seen again. Stockwell claims to see Hicks encountering a youngster accompanied by an older man two hours or so before his disappearance and repeats the same story about him being asked to find a missing dog. Stockwell believed that Hicks was killed on one location and moved to another – a place where there was water. He claimed those responsible for Reece's death also killed Kevin Hicks. The older man he described was now dead but the younger of the perpetrators was still alive.

It's obviously all totally circumstantial, and stories by psychics such as this are often ridiculed, but the facts are there and whilst it would be easy for me to manipulate them to fit my story, the links between the things Stockwell described point towards Derek (Splodgegun), his scary sidekick, and possibly even Rob. As I said, he was well-known in the area thanks to his football activities, but what happened to him in the period between me fleeing that train station back in early 1981 and these murders four and five years later is anyone's guess. Certainly Stockwell's description of a man well known and ridiculed by local children fits the bill, but it was the trench coat that really did it for me. I guess I'll never know just what I escaped when I fled that night.

I'm obviously nor accusing anyone of anything and in my experiences with Rob he always looked out for me, this could of course is all conjecture.

For many years I accepted what I feared Derek was doing as being a hazard of youth football. I remember telling work colleagues about him many years before the stories surfaced about child sex abuse in the junior game and they found it simply comical. Only when some of the recent stories have come to light did much of it ring true and after hearing some of the details revealed by Tony Stockwell in these unsolved cases, the true extent of what may have happened could be even more horrific, but will never be known.

ABOUT THE AUTHOR

Merv Payne was born in Clapham, south London in 1972. During the height of the football fanzine boom of the late 80s he co-produced a south London fanzine called Don't Panic. After moving to Manchester in 1992 he worked for various publishing and design agencies. He has had various articles published in national newspapers and magazines as well as online at Sabotage Times as well as being a regular contributor to the official Millwall match programme.

58056360R00133

Made in the USA
Columbia, SC
17 May 2019